NONPROFIT STRATEGY:
A PHASE-BASED APPROACH TO RELEVANCE, IMPACT, AND SUSTAINABILITY

Michael E. Stone, Ph.D.
Spring 2020

NONPROFIT STRATEGY: A PHASE-BASED APPROACH
TO RELEVANCE, IMPACT, AND SUSTAINABILITY
Copyright © 2020 by Michael E. Stone, Ph.D.

ISBN 978-0-578-73389-0

Printed in USA

TABLE OF CONTENTS

FOREWORD

Strategic planning is arguably one of the most respected nonprofit management disciplines. It is a rare best-practice inventory that doesn't include strategic planning as a must. Yet there are as many approaches to planning as there are nonprofit executives, board members or consultants who lead them. Into this ubiquitous field comes Mike Stone's book Nonprofit Strategy, a fresh and innovative take on nonprofit strategic planning. Stone's book, and its practical, nuanced approach, arrives on the scene just as nonprofits face one of the most challenging times in recent history. Navigating the future, near- and longer-term, is what this book is about.

Nonprofit Strategy is the right blend of practice and theory. It is down-to-earth enough to be a DIY guide for nonprofits conducting their own planning processes. It will be a resource for funders seeking strategic context for grantmaking investments and programmatic direction. Nonprofit consultants, too, will appreciate its solid framework and the scaffolding it provides for their own planning techniques.

Along with an emphasis on both strategy and planning, three seminal concepts undergird Stone's book. Logic modeling, developed in the late 1960s as a hypothesized method to anticipate a chain of cause and effects and outcomes that might follow; the MacMillan Matrix, developed in the 1970s to help nonprofits make program decisions; and lifecycle theory which recognizes that nonprofits develop in stages rather than come into existence fully mature. For his lifecycle framework, Stone uses my book Nonprofit Lifecycles, Stage-based Wisdom for Nonprofit Capacity, published in 2002. Nonprofit Lifecycles defines and describes the seven developmental stages nonprofits may go through in their maturation process... Idea, Startup, Growth, Maturity, Decline, Turnaround, Terminal ... matching capacity challenges and setting expectations consistent with each distinct stage.

The Nonprofit Lifecycles Institute I founded in 2015 has an impressive roster of Lifecycle Capacity Consultants from throughout the US and Canada. Each brings a unique set of skills to their lifecycle work. With Nonprofit Strategy, Mike Stone brings a profound appreciation of lifecycle theory to the subject of nonprofit strategy. This is the first written work I have seen that codifies and couples lifecycle theory with strategic planning.

Nonprofit Strategy is actually Stone's second book. His first, From the Inside Out: A Nonprofit's Guide to Meaningful Strategy was published in 2017. It summarizes much of what Stone learned through his years in higher education, in philanthropy as a foundation program director and CEO, and now as a consultant.

I read nonprofit management books for two reasons: to learn something that extends my theoretical knowledge, and to gain ideas and techniques that apply to my work. Nonprofit Strategy gave me both. I learned something new in each chapter.

As it happened, around the time I was reading this book's manuscript, I was also advising my niece on a nonprofit she is starting to provide services to foster families. It had been a long time since I had consulted with an Idea-stage founder on how to get her concept incorporated, draft a mission statement, recruit a board and develop articles of incorporation. It was my good fortune to find a chapter in Stone's book on just that: Idea-stage to Startup: Clarifying Aspiration. That chapter, and several that follow, leads with a very relatable case study before providing insights and tools for strategy development at this particular stage.

This book isn't all lifecycles and case studies, though. The first and last chapters deftly discuss strategic positioning and highlight the role external and internal patterns and trends play in strategy development. Nonprofits and consultants will find this a very valuable mental framework for analysis while planning. The explanation and use of logic modeling throughout the book will be appreciated by funders, especially by strategic learning officers and program evaluators.

It's been nearly twenty years since I wrote Nonprofit Lifecycles. Back then, I had no idea whether it would stand the test of time. Yet here we are twenty years later with sales still steady, and demand continuing. I predict this same kind of shelf-life for Nonprofit Strategy. Stone's book will be a timeless gift to the nonprofit sector.

There's an old saying, we stand on the shoulders of those who've come before. For me, this adage flipped around when I read Stone's work. There is no greater testament than to have your work advanced and elevated by those who come after. This is what Mike Stone has done in Nonprofit Strategy. He has taken nonprofit lifecycle theory, along with logic modeling and the MacMillan Matrix, and elevated each of these concepts with a fresh spin and the added lens of strategy.

It is always an honor to write the Foreword for a book you believe in. I've had that privilege several times before, but always with authors who were known colleagues. This time is different, I have never personally met or worked with Mike Stone. And yet, it is he who has written the book I will now proudly promote as a companion to my book, Nonprofit Lifecycles.

Enjoy Nonprofit Strategy and watch for it to become the new go-to for nonprofits, consultants and funders seeking to strengthen the sector through solid strategy and a stage-based approach to strategic planning.

Susan Kenny Stevens, Ph.D.
Author, Nonprofit Lifecycles
June 2020

PREFACE

The nonprofit sector has had its share of trends and fads. Sometimes it is a piece of jargon that has merit but whose underlying power gets diluted by overuse and misuse (collaboration, anyone?). Occasionally, however, something comes along that is so clear and of such practical value that it becomes absorbed into our default mindsets about nonprofit organizations. Three examples come to mind: The first is the MacMillan Matrix,[1] a tool developed in the 1970s to help nonprofits make program decisions based on a number of strategic criteria. It has been replicated on numerous occasions, but in my opinion, the value of the original has yet to be duplicated.

The second example of useful tools is the logic model. I spent ten years teaching nonprofits how to construct and use logic models through a local private foundation. People either loved or hated them; few were anywhere in the middle. On one end of the continuum were those who are hard-wired to see the big picture. On the other end were those whose passion was for rolling up their sleeves and doing the work on the ground. The fortunate organizations are those with a mix of both types.

The third example of the nonprofit triumvirate of useful tools, and an advanced organizer for this book, is the Nonprofit

---

[1] Developed by Ian MacMillan at the Wharton School of Business.

Lifecycles framework.[2] I find the framework to be invaluable in my work as a consultant, in that it places challenges facing nonprofits in the proper context. The result is that these challenges are recognized as natural growing pains associated with an organization on the move.

As noted by Susan Kenny Stevens, strategic planning for nonprofits must align with the organization's current circumstances. To quote Susan: The starting point matters. While the Lifecycles framework is rooted in the minds of many practitioners and consultants, the concept of strategic planning has no similar anchoring framework.

Clearly, strategic planning in the nonprofit sector needs an anchor. Because of its own evolution (developed in the military, adopted by corporations, then imported into the nonprofit sector), nonprofits find themselves trying to force the square peg into the round hole. Moving the Lifecycle Stages framework "above the table legs" will bring about three benefits:

First, it will extend its utility by integrating a larger set of questions that organizations should address in planning. Second, it brings greater focus and clarity to the process of strategic development by placing it in the context of the Lifecycle Stages. And third, it will provide a more nuanced view of the capacity needs of nonprofits within the five areas in the

---

[2] Susan Kenny Stevens, Ph.D., *Nonprofit Lifecycles: Stage-Based Wisdom for Nonprofit Capacity* (Stagewise Enterprises, Inc., 2001:2008).

Lifecycle Stages framework. In other words, the strategic direction can shape the capacity needs of the organization.

My hopes and beliefs are that integrating the Lifecycle Stages framework into my approach to nonprofit strategy will strengthen both processes and, most importantly, will strengthen nonprofits.

INTRODUCTION:

The Nature of Nonprofit Strategy

Words matter. More specifically, the meaning that we attach to words matter. The problem, as we know too well, is that the meaning of the words we use rests in the separate minds of the speaker and the listener. Simply, words that we all know and use regularly may not mean the same thing to each of us. Such is the case with strategy.

The challenge for nonprofits is not that they don't know how to construct a written strategic plan. To the contrary, nonprofits are quite good at developing lists of things that need be done. The problem is that the term strategy has become inherently ambiguous by its use as a stand-in word for a lot of different types and levels of activity. Consider the three uses of the concept within the context of a single organization aimed at one specific goal:

- "Our strategic goal is to become less dependent on government funding."

- "Our fundraising strategy is built around obtaining more major gifts."

- "We need to develop strategies for identifying and nurturing potential donors."

In the most general sense, I define strategy as the exercise of intentional choice regarding the use of organizational resources. One requirement of successful strategy development and execution is the ability to differentiate between the two levels of strategy. As we move from vision to action, I recommend we sharpen our language about strategy to encompasses two levels of activity.

- Macro-Level Strategy is big-picture thinking that is concerned with the positioning of the organization in the long-term. Macro-level strategy is built around a small number of questions that are based on the lifecycle stage of the nonprofit. We will explore those questions in subsequent chapters.

- Micro-Level Strategy is about short-term implementation. The vantage point for micro-level strategy is one that provides clear line of sight to the daily operational and program decisions and activities that will move the organization in the direction it has chosen for itself.

Figure 1 shows the movement from macro-level strategy (which is long-term and aimed at movement); to micro-level strategy, which is short-term and focused on activities). As we work down the pyramid from planning to implementation, we encounter a key transition point in the form of strategic priorities, a concept we will address in a later chapter.

Figure 1: From Macro-Strategy to Micro-Strategy

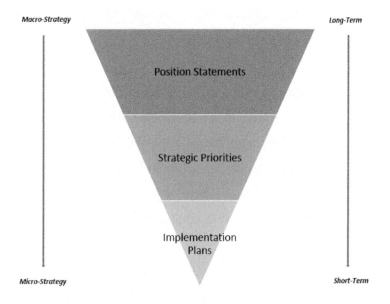

How Nonprofit Strategy is Different

There are aspects of traditional for-profit strategy that have been good for the nonprofit sector. The most beneficial aspect of for-profit strategy is that it brought attention to such concepts as core competencies, markets, and profit margins. But the wholesale application of for-profit strategy to nonprofits is not the solution. The very nature of nonprofit strategy differs from for-profit strategy on a number of basic assumptions. Those key assumptions are described below.

Nonprofit strategy is both driven by and constrained within a social mission. The overriding goal of a for-profit company is to stay in business, usually by expanding markets or expanding product lines in order to increase profits. This is not the case for nonprofits, which operate under the influence of a governor of sorts, its social mission, which keeps the organization from straying too far from its founding purpose.

Nonprofits do not operate within the traditional open market. The reality is that nonprofits exist because the traditional open market exchange between buyer and seller does not work in this setting. You will know if there are too many restaurants in your town when some of them close their doors. Whereas consumer demand alone will support a for-profit, this is not true for nonprofits. To remain viable, a nonprofit must have both client demand and third parties willing to pay the nonprofit to meet that demand.

Bigger is not always better. The economic reality is that many nonprofits lose money on every client served (which is why the traditional market will not support the work and consequently why fundraising is so important). For these nonprofits, reaching more people, a common strategic goal, means losing even more money. Strategic growth, a more appropriate goal, may mean doing less, perhaps for fewer people, but with greater precision and intensity. Greater mission impact is always better.

The nonprofit sector flourishes when individual organizations complement, rather than compete. I stand by the assertion that the nonprofit sector is stronger, and individual nonprofits more viable, when each nonprofit is able to identify its place in the larger system—and stay within its lane. This does require that individual nonprofits differentiate themselves from similar providers, much like for-profit companies. But the purpose of differentiation for a nonprofit is not to put the other providers out of business. Rather, nonprofit differentiation is about clarifying to potential clients, funders, and collaborators how its fits within the larger network or system.

Many have argued that nonprofits need to think more like for-profit businesses. Well, yes and no. No, for all of the reasons described above. Yes, in that nonprofits need to be reminded that they are a business entity before they are a tax-exempt organization. A business must be profitable to endure, even if we prefer to call it something else in the nonprofit sector. And, to my amazement, there are still nonprofit board members who wear the low salaries they offer as a badge of honor, a reflection of their commitment to the greater mission of the organization. The demand for talent is the same regardless of sector. Can you imagine the board of directors of a major corporation seeking out a bargain-priced CEO?

Strategic Positioning for Nonprofits

There is a wide area of shared space between the for-profit and nonprofit sectors when it comes to strategy development. The approach to strategy that I believe has the most utility is the approach known as strategic positioning.[3] In short, strategic positioning entails finding a space in the market where your organization can be successful, whether that is by feeding the hungry or producing widgets. As we will see, what differs between the two sectors are a) the definition of success and b) the variables that go into the formulation of the desired strategic position.

From a strategic standpoint, the essential (and existential) challenges facing all nonprofits are relevance,

---

[3] Several authors have written about this approach, most notably Michael Porter, Henry Mintzberg, and Thomas McLaughlin.

impact, and sustainability. Relevance means that the mission of the nonprofit is aimed at some form of social good that is considered to be of value to people outside the organization. Demonstrating impact requires that the nonprofit operate under a clearly articulated theory of change and is able to substantiate some form and degree of change. The pursuit of sustainability is the reality check in nonprofit strategy development in that it forces the organization to weigh trade-offs between mission and margin.

The guiding question that drives nonprofit strategy development is straightforward: how do we position our organization to be able to produce relevant community impact in a sustainable manner? The strategic position of a nonprofit encompasses three areas:

- The Program Position, which is a description of what you will do, for whom in what circumstances, and to what end.

- The Market Position, which describes how your organization will relate to and differentiate itself from others in your domain.[4]

---

[4] A domain could be defined *geographically* (e.g., a community center), by *industry* (e.g., the child welfare system), or by *demographics* (e.g., low-income families).

- The Resource Position, which describes what your organization believes is the most sustainable mix of funding sources and types.

The formulation of a strategic position is not the product of wishful thinking about the way things should be, nor does it need to include something big and bold. Rather, a strategic position emerges out of informed and reflective discussions around three questions:

1. What do we aspire to be?
2. What does our community need us to be?
3. What do we have the ability to be?

The core competency in the strategic positioning is pattern recognition.[5] A pattern occurs when a trend takes on a recognizable form. Like judging the shape of the river, pattern recognition requires a wider view. For example, program data may show a ten-year decline in participation. Viewed through a wider lens, however, a pattern emerges that shows that program funding tends to run in cycles that correspond to state elections through which the balance of power shifts from one party to the other.

---

[5] Henry Mintzberg, *Tracking Strategies: Toward a General Theory*. (Oxford University Press, 2007).

In short, developing a strategic position requires the ability to analyze and make sense of the patterns from the past. As noted by Henry Mintzberg, patterns are both intentional and emergent.[6] Emergent patterns are the result of the aggregation of a number of unconnected or unrelated decisions over time. It is for this reason that I often begin strategic planning by having the organization look backward to discover those embedded patterns of decisions, milestones, successes, and failures that brought the nonprofit to where it is today. Examples of emergent patterns include the following:

- We are more successful in new ventures when we have collaborating partners.

- Our outcomes are best for those clients with the greatest need.

- Though we consider ourselves to be communitywide in scope, the vast majority of our clients are referred to us by the courts.

Without an understanding of trends and patterns in the internal and external environments, the result is likely to be nothing more than an unattainable vision supported by a list of

---

[6] Ibid.

unachievable tasks.[7] Once established, the strategic position of the nonprofit needs to be assessed in its entirety. In determining the viability of the strategic position, the nonprofit should look for the following characteristics:

- Individual feasibility: What is the likelihood that each of the three components can be attained on their own?

- Internal consistency: Is there is a logic that connects the three components into an integrated vision for the organization?

- Mutually supporting: Will the attainment of one component contribute to the attainment of the others?

On the whole, the ideal strategic position for a nonprofit is one that: a) will allow the organization to create relevant community impact; b) builds on the unique or distinguishing qualities of the organization; and, c) will attract the human and financial resources it needs to meet the mission.

---

[7] A version of this statement is attributed to Peter Drucker.

Strategy Across the Lifecycle Stages

As a former career counselor and a parent of two children, I have had numerous conversations with people about their hopes, dreams, and aspirations. For my own children, the discussions were basic (and usually short!) and were centered around what they wanted to be when they grow up. As a college career counselor, the discussions were more sophisticated and refined. Coming off of an internship, the college students would be asked to reflect on what they learned from the hands-on experience, both about themselves and the world of work. Working with mid-career adults, the discussions tended to be much more reflective and centered on finding deeper meaning through work.

At one level, all three categories of people were after the same outcome: meaningful, interesting work. But I would not ask a fifty-year-old accountant what they wanted to be when they grow up; nor would I ask a third-grader to reflect on what school has taught them about their prospects for a meaningful career. Being an effective career counselor and parent meant that I had to ask the right questions at the right time.

Such is the case with nonprofit strategy. The goal is always strategic positioning. However, the particular considerations that go into the development of a desired strategic position change depending on the starting position of that particular nonprofit. More specifically, the questions that guide the planning process will differ based on the developmental phase of the organization. For that, we turn to the Lifecycle Stages framework.

Stage Theory[8]

Stage theory is a set of assumptions that human development is marked by critical junctures and milestones that result in qualitative changes in capabilities and characteristic behaviors at each phase of life.[9] A defining characteristic of stage theory is the idea that movement from one phase to another requires the individual to master a set of specific challenges or circumstances. While adhering to these basic tenets of stage theory, the nonprofit Lifecycle Stages framework offers a few caveats:

- There is no exact number of lifecycle stages as agreed upon by scholars and practitioners of organizational development.

- Not all organizations go through all of the stages and, if they do, the movement is not always sequential.

- Movement across the lifecycles is neither age nor size dependent.

---

[8] The contents of this section are drawn from Susan Kenny Stevens, Ph.D., *Nonprofit Lifecycles: Stage-Based Wisdom for Nonprofit Capacity* (Stagewise Enterprises, Inc. 2001; 2008).
[9] Kenney Stevens, *Nonprofit Lifecycles*, page 17.

A summary of the seven phases presented in the Lifecycles Stages framework is presented in Figure 2 below:

Figure 2: Nonprofit Lifecycle Stages

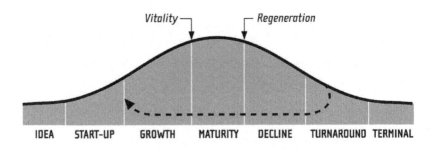

© 2001. Susan Kenny Stevens, Ph.D. *Nonprofit Lifecycles: Stage-based Wisdom for Nonprofit Capacity.*

Used with author permission.

The Lifestyle Stages Framework

Figure 2 provides an overview of the strategic phases that align with each Lifecycle Stages. Each cell contains the broad mandate in each of the three areas of nonprofit strategy relative each of the Lifecycle Stages. In addition, each lifecycle stage corresponds to a phase of strategic positioning and the key attribute that governs that particular phase. A nonprofit moving from Idea to Startup, for example, is considered to be in the aspirational phase of strategic positioning. The key attribute of strategy in the aspirational phase is clarity of intent. At the other extreme are the organizations moving from Decline to Turnaround, which requires a new strategic position created through a process of refocusing efforts, attention, and resources. It is worth noting that any nonprofit at any stage can move toward Decline. The lesson is that even nonprofits that start out strong must remain nimble and responsive as things around them change.

Though not explicit in the case studies, strategic positioning at each lifecycle stage builds on the strategic positioning phases that have preceded. For example, the case study of the organization featured in the section on strategic positioning at the Mature stage focuses only on the tasks associated with that stage. In reality, it may be necessary to go back to the beginning to clarify intent (Startup) and assess the boundaries implemented (Growth) before addressing the tasks specific to the Mature stage.

Strategic Capacity Building

A second aspect of the Lifecycle Stages framework that informs this book is the breakdown of capacity-building into key areas of the nonprofit. In simple terms, capacity-building is another term for organizational capability and performance.[10] As

---

[10] Stevens, p. 12.

shown in Figure 3, capacity-building strengthens the table legs that support the programs and ultimately, the mission of the organization. The areas that make up the legs of the table are management, governance, the business model, and administrative systems.

Figure 3: The Capacity-Building Model

At one level, the capacity needs of the nonprofit are general and universal. For example, there is a natural and logical evolution of board governance as an organization moves from Startup toward Maturity. The shorthand version of this evolution is moving from a "working board" to a "policy board".[11] However, capacity needs may also be specific to the strategic aspirations of the nonprofit. A nonprofit seeking to revise its resource position (say, by shifting from foundation grants to charitable giving) will look for specific attributes that support the shift as it considers prospective board members. It is important to note that the emphasis on resource development does not replace the general governance needs of the organization. Rather, strategic targeting of board members will enhance the overall governance strength of the organization.

---

[11] I put quotation marks around these because the reality is that every board works and deals with policy at some level. The differentiator is how deeply involved the board is in the two areas.

LAYOUT OF THE BOOK

The remainder of the book is dedicated to the integration of the Lifecycle Stages framework with the approach to nonprofit strategy known as strategic positioning. Each of the next four chapters provides a case study application of strategic planning utilizing the Lifecycle Stages framework to identify the corresponding strategic phase of the nonprofit. Chapter 2 highlights a nonprofit preparing to move from the Idea stage to the Startup stage.

Chapter 3 features a nonprofit facing the challenges of managing its activities while building its capacity at the Growth stage. Chapter 4 takes an in-depth look at an organization at the Mature stage attempting to maintain its historic purpose in light of significant external changes. Finally, Chapter 5 will track the deliberations undertaken by an organization firmly in the Decline stage and looking for a viable Turnaround strategy.

Chapter 6 shifts focus by examining case studies where strategic positioning of an organization focalizes the capacity-building challenges typically faced by non-profits in each stage.

Though brief, the chapter is intended to close the loop that combines strategy, lifecycles, and capacity-building into a mutually-enforcing process. The last part of Chapter 6 provides a template for a framework document that encompasses strategic priorities (i.e., those activities that advance the efforts toward the desired strategic position) and the capacity priorities (i.e., those activities that strengthen the legs of the table).

Table 1: Strategic Position by Lifecycle Stage

	Idea/Startup	Growth	Maturity	Decline/Turnaround
STRATEGIC PHASE	**Aspiration**	**Adaptation**	**Affirmation**	**Reposition**
KEY ATTRIBUTE	**Clarity**	**Discipline**	**Resilience**	**Focus**
Relevance	*Substantiate* External Demand	*Respond* to Emergent Demand	*Identify* Essential Characteristics	*Realign* Mission Priorities
Impact	*Clarify* the Theory of Change	*Refine* the Program Model	*Assess* the Strategic Value of Programs	*Narrow* the Scope of Impact
Sustainability	*Establish* the Business Model	*Revise* the Business Model	*Preserve* Long-term Assets	*Reestablish* a Business Model

CHAPTER 1: FROM IDEA TO STARTUP
Clarifying Aspirations

Early in my consulting career, I received a phone call from a young couple who had just graduated from college and wanted to take what they felt was a call to personal ministry and combine it with the stability of an incorporated business entity. In other words, they wanted to start a nonprofit. The purpose of the nonprofit would be to use street hockey as the basis of a youth ministry program. The couple wanted to purchase a van or trailer, stock it with street hockey equipment, travel to different neighborhoods, and set up the field. The youth would come, they believed, and the attraction of street hockey would provide an opening for the couple to reach deeper into the lives of youth with their ministerial message.

My initial conversation was rather informal, one of those "brain picking" sessions in which consultants often find themselves. In truth, I was skeptical of the idea going in. I had enough experience to recognize the difficulties that arise when a personal ministry becomes a public charity. To the unexperienced, becoming a nonprofit seems like a sure-fire way to get the money they need to do what they want to do. Anyone can write a grant, after all. This couple, like many others, did not understand that a 501(c)(3) designation is, in effect, nothing more than a hunting license for grant seekers and fundraisers.

Given the opportunity for a re-do, my approach would be much more formal by framing my probing strategic questions in the context of lifecycle stage development. [12]

Startup Strategy

The vignette above is a familiar one to many of us. People believe that their idea, because it feels like the right thing to do, will happen through sheer will, determination, and faith. Sometimes, they are right; small ideas can blossom into large, successful organizations over time. But sometimes, even the grandest ideas never make it out of the starting gate. There are numerous reasons for this, though the final blow is usually related to an imbalance of revenue and expenses. The actual case, however, often is deeply embedded in the core assumptions about the relevance of the program.

In reality, the idea, vision, or calling that compels someone to start a nonprofit is nothing more than a grand hypothesis. Becoming incorporated and receiving the tax-exempt status are, frankly, not that difficult to achieve. Achieving these designations says nothing about the likelihood that the organization will create impact and find financial equilibrium. This is not intended to diminish the value of the idea, nor should it dampen the passion of the individuals who came up with the idea. The nonprofit organization is nothing but the structural

---

[12] As of this writing, the Lamp lighter Hockey is in its fifth year and with an expanded curriculum. Congratulations to them.

representation of an idea that someone believes will address a problem or need in the world.

Clarity is important in all aspects of strategy and throughout the lifecycles of a nonprofit. For a nonprofit at the startup stage, clarity is essential. The priority objective of startup strategy development is to clarify the elements that will make up the case you will make to external audiences for why the organization should exist in the first place. Convincing someone that they should support the organization, which is often the first impulse, comes later and depends on the quality of the first task. But, first things first.

Below is an exploration of strategy development for Caring Communities, a newly minted nonprofit organization trying to move from the Idea stage to the Startup stage. The development of the strategy will follow the three dimensions of strategy presented in the introduction: relevance, impact, and sustainability.

Relevance: To Whom Do You Matter?

Relevance means that the founding purpose of the nonprofit is aimed at some form of social good that is considered to be of value to people outside the founder or the organization. In plain language, relevance is a function of the following:

- What problem are you attempting to solve?

- To whom will this problem matter?
- How will your activities benefit them?

David spent several years as a direct service provider in group homes for adults with developmental disabilities before founding Caring Communities. While he enjoyed the work, he became increasingly frustrated with many aspects of the system. First, he felt that client placements were based on availability more than the needs of the individual client family. Second, he noticed that the constant turnover of direct service providers disrupted the continuity of relationships that, in his opinion, formed the foundation for a quality living experience.

After much research and discussions with families, David devised an entirely new approach to housing for individuals with developmental disabilities. In short, David developed a program and a financial model that, in effect, would give full control over housing options to the families, including the floor plan of the houses that were to be built. When David presented the model to families of developmentally disabled adults, the response was overwhelming, and the wait list grew to over 80 families before funding was secured for the first house.

Analysis: Relevance

The first strategic challenge facing Caring Communities is the same as it is for other nonprofits in the Startup stage: how do you establish the relevance of your new or proposed organization? To review, here are the questions to be answered when establishing organizational relevance: What problem are you trying to solve? To whom will this problem matter? How will your activities benefit them?

One note of clarification is in order before we proceed. The idea of "solving a problem" is not the most accurate way of describing the purpose of some nonprofits. The symphony, for example, enriches life more than it solves a problem that can be remedied only by attending a concert. (You could argue, and many people have, that not experiencing the arts is a problem). For our purposes, I use the phrase "solving a problem" in the most general way to capture the idea of the founding purpose of a nonprofit.

David's approach to the problem of housing for disabled individuals came from his experience working with the people for whom the benefits are intended. David responded to this external demand (in this case, for more control over housing options and decisions) by devising an entirely new way of approaching the problem. Specifically, the relevance formula for Caring Communities is as follows:

- The activities of the organization matter to adults with developmental disabilities and to their families.

- The benefit to the adults with disabilities is the opportunity to live in a community of their choosing. The benefit to families is the alleviation of worries about what happens to their adult children when the parents are no longer around.

At its core, the relevance criterion rests on the difference between unmet need and demand. We can understand the difference between the two by considering 'who says'. The demands of the beneficiaries are baked into the Caring Communities cake. Families of adults with developmental disabilities need more control over the long-term housing situations. Who says? The families themselves. Caring Communities is a response to the demand emanating from those most affected by the problem.

Establishing relevance at the Idea stage is not about trying to convince everyone that they should care about what you have identified as an unmet need. Rather, establishing relevance is about gauging the size of the population that you have reason to believe is likely to care as much as you do. As we shall see, the importance of understanding those who share your passion extends well beyond recruiting program participants. If we know one thing about nonprofit fundraising, it is that who cares is who pays...and not everyone will care. The issue of funding will be taken up in greater detail in the sustainability section of the strategy model.

Impact: How Will You Make a Difference?

Demonstrating impact requires two things of a nonprofit. First, the nonprofit must show that it is operating under a clearly articulated theory of change.[13] This is the big picture thinking about how the planned activities will contribute to the intended impact. Second, the nonprofit must be able to substantiate some form and degree of change that is tied to its program activities. In other words, success occurs when the behavior of the participants changes in a positive direction.

The intended purpose of a logic model is aimed exactly at these two requirements: it makes explicit how a nonprofit believes it can best use its resources to bring about mission impact; and it identifies the information the nonprofit will gather to substantiate the desired change.

From the perspective of organizational development, evaluation is aimed at program improvement and rooted in ongoing learning. Unless struck by an inordinate amount of luck and some impeccable timing, most nonprofits do not get it exactly right the first time. What matters most is not just how close you may come to meeting your programmatic expectations,

---

[13] *Logic model* and *theory of change* have been used interchangeably. The focus of both is on the underlying logic that connects specific activities to certain desired outcomes.

but how well you understand why you fell short. What is a bad idea—a good idea poorly implemented? A good idea, properly implemented, but needing more time to gain traction?

Once the logic model is constructed, it becomes the framework in which the nonprofit gauges its progress. More specifically, comprehensive evaluation of mission impact requires that you evaluate each aspect of the logic model. Those aspects are:

- The underlying assumptions and expectations about the approach (the Logic).
- The type and number of anticipated program activities (the Implementation).
- The intended benefits to participants (the Outcomes).

The format for the logic model that I prefer is adapted from the work of Schon and Argyles. [14] Their basic formula is that a practitioner engages in selected actions (A) aimed at individuals in specific situations (S) to bring about a desired consequence (C). For the sake of simplicity, think of the formula as $A \rightarrow S = C$. Following this formula, the logic model for Caring Communities would look like this:

---

[14] The premise is that professionals make decisions every day based on an implicit theory of what will work in a given situation to bring about the desire result (a phenomenon referred to as *theory of practice*).

Table 2: Caring Communities Theory of Change

Action	Situation	Consequence
Provide affordable housing options	Families of adults with DD	Peace of mind
Community living options	Adults with DD	Stability, meaningful life

Theory of Change: Analysis

The Logic

The core logic underlying Caring Communities is that giving families choice among a wider range of housing options will satisfy the emotional needs of parents while offering a higher quality of life for adults living in the houses. The value of a simple logic model like the one adapted above is that it makes the implicit theory of change more explicit. The process of constructing the logic model will uncover gaps in thinking or erroneous thinking, in addition to identifying the key assumptions on which the logic of the program rests. With a clear expression of what you will do and why it matters, the next step is to focus on the anticipated scope of the program.

The Implementation

Planning and tracking implementation activities is important for two main reasons. First, the implementation plan communicates to external audiences an estimate of the scope and depth of the activities you plan to provide. Is it a one-time workshop to raise awareness of the benefits of fitness? Or, will the program foster longer-term relationships that can serve as the basis of the gradual introduction of new information and activities?

Second, implementation estimations provide a baseline of expectations against which actual performance can be compared, conclusions drawn, and program improvements made. This difference in depth and scope will become more vital in the outcomes section, but it is equally valuable in setting expectations for what might be considered the productivity level of the program during one full cycle. Caring Communities, because of the complexity and inter-relatedness of the various program components, is less likely to be defined by a specific period of time, such as an academic year of the summer months.

What does a reasonable implementation plan and timeline look like for Caring Communities? As a reminder, the implementation plan within the context of a theory of change is high-level and general, not ground-level and granular. That is, we know that each of the implementation steps listed above will require their own plan of execution (who calls whom, by when, etc.). For planning purposes, it is more reasonable and appropriate to identify project milestones. An implementation plan for the first full cycle of Caring Communities may look something like this:

Milestone	Timeframe
Land identified for purchase	Within six months of launch
Families selected	Within one year of launch
Money raised	Within eighteen months of launch
First house opens	Within two years of launch

To this point, we have completed two important steps toward the main task of demonstrating impact. It is important to keep in mind that the theory of change (as represented by the logic model) for an organization moving from Ideal to Startup represents aspirations and intentions. It is unrealistic to expect that a nonprofit will be able to actually demonstrate meaningful outcomes over the course of one program cycle. For this reason, the theory of change includes a range of outcomes from short-term to long-term. The task for the nonprofit is to identify the chain of outcomes, then decide which should result directly from their program and, consequently, which will be held accountable.

The Outcomes

Typically, outcomes are thought of as a chain of positive benefits, each built upon preceding benefits. The breakdown of outcomes is as follows:

- Short-term outcomes are in the form of new information, changing attitudes, or deeper understanding. For example, the hope of the authors is that by reading this book, nonprofit professionals will think of strategy in a new, more useful way.

- Intermediate outcomes are the new behaviors that result from the new information, attitudes, or understanding. To continue the aforementioned example, the authors hope that readers will change the way they approach strategy development within their own organizations from what they learned by reading this book.

- Long-term outcomes indicate a better overall condition for the people who participated in the program or activity. The long-term hope of the authors is that by learning new ways to approach strategy, nonprofit professionals will be more effective in their own strategic planning, which will (eventually) make them more relevant, impactful, and sustainable.

This is an example of the chain of outcomes that every nonprofit should be able to construct about the intended impact of their programs. The success of a particular program doesn't depend on the ability to provide evidence of outcomes across the entire chain. To the contrary: selecting appropriate outcomes from the chain of logic requires the discipline to limit the claims of impact to those that are, well, logical. The following factors should guide the identification and measurement of appropriate outcomes:

- Potency: What is the intensity of engagement with the program participants? There is a difference, for example, between the results of a one-time information session and from an ongoing series of activities.

- Control: How much influence do you have over the conditions that affect your program participants when they are not with you or your organization?

- Timing: How long do you expect it will take for the benefits to materialize?

Let's imagine that I, as the author, want to assess the impact of reading this book. To this end, I devise a brief survey that is sent to individuals three months after they purchase the book. What questions do I ask if I want to judge whether or not I have achieved my desired outcome of strengthening nonprofit organizations? Following my own chain of outcomes, I am likely to want answers to the following questions:

1. What did you learn or what do you understand differently about nonprofit strategy?

2. How were you able to apply what you learned to your own organization?

3. How is your organization more relevant, impactful, or sustainable because of your application of the concepts presented in the book?

From the perspective of potency, it is safe to assume that I would not have bothered to write the book if I didn't believe that the information had the potential to strengthen, or in some cases transform nonprofit organizations. However, a significant mitigating factor in desire for long-term impact is my lack of control. I can support and encourage but cannot make anyone do anything differently within their organization after reading the book. (Every consultant reading this is nodding their heads in vigorous agreement).

Given this inherent limitation, how can I assess the value of our book? It is entirely reasonable to expect positive responses to question 1. If enough respondents indicate that they did not learn much from the book (i.e., I failed to achieve even the short-term outcome), there is little value in pressing on with the other questions. I should hold ourselves 100% accountable for my ability to change the way people think about strategy.

Assuming positive responses to the first question, it is appropriate to at least probe the second question. However, the balance of accountability shifts at this point (let's say 50/50 for the sake of discussion). On one hand, I cannot make anyone act on what they learned from the book. On the other hand, it is reasonable to expect that if the information is useful enough, readers would want to do something with that new information.

You have probably beat me to the conclusion that there is no value in asking about the overall standing of the organization three months after the purchase of the book. There will be a time in the future when it will make sense to ask people who have been working with the model for a number of years to reflect on the differences they have seen in their organizations as a result. It is simply unreasonable to expect such deep impact any sooner.

In light of these considerations, a positive evaluation of the impact of this book would look something like this:

- 92% of readers were able identify at two concepts or principles they learned from the book.

- Of those 92% who learned something from the book, 85% were able to identify at least two processes or activities they have implemented as a result of the book.

Based on these findings, a reasonable person would conclude that the book has the intended impact, even though the long-term impact has yet to be substantiated. This is the challenge facing Caring Communities when it comes to demonstrating impact.

Recall that demand from the intended beneficiaries is what brought Caring Communities into being in the first place. For David, only time will tell if his approach results in a higher quality of life for residents and less worry for parents. The best he can do in the meantime is ensure that he continually responds to the demands and expectations of families as circumstances change. Much like the Field of Dreams, David knows that if he builds it correctly, families will benefit.

Sustainability: How Will You Maintain Support for Your Work?

I often begin strategy training sessions with the following statement: "If serving the homeless were to become profitable on its own, then there would be a saturation in the market of for-profit providers competing to serve the homeless." This is in no way is a criticism of the profit motive in general or of for-profit providers who have moved into what once was the exclusive domain of nonprofits (think hospice care and disabilities services). Rather, it serves to remind folks in the nonprofit sector (especially board members) that they are not in Kansas anymore. Capturing more of the market is a common approach to declining revenues in the for-profit sector. However, in an environment of subsidized service, "growth" can actually deepen the financial hole you are trying to fill. It speaks to the old business adage: if you lose money on every transaction, you can't make it up in volume!

Simply put, nonprofit service providers exist because the traditional exchange of service for fees in the open market does not work.[15] Nonprofits wanting to expand must not only find more clients, they also must find someone willing to pay the nonprofit to serve those new clients. This reliance on third-party payors is the defining characteristic of nonprofit economics and which makes sustainability planning a crucial element of nonprofit strategy.

Earlier in this chapter, I introduced the idea that "who cares is who pays…and not everyone will care." Research into nonprofit funding has identified a few key trends and patterns that support this colloquial aphorism. For example, the National Center on Nonprofit Enterprise has shown that stable nonprofits tend to have one primary source that is supported by two or three

---

[15] This is not to suggest that fee-for-service is not relevant to nonprofits. But even the symphony and the ballet, for example, have to raise charitable dollars to subsidize the actual cost of providing performances to patrons.

supplemental sources.[16] Further, they note that the greatest predictor of sustainability is the reliability of the primary source, with government funding being the least reliable and individual charitable contributions the most reliable. Between the two lie foundation grants.

The second key pattern is that nonprofits eventually settle into one of a handful of meta-models of funding. The landing spot for any particular nonprofit is not a matter of choice; rather, funding models correspond to the type of benefit created by the nonprofit, which is then tied to those individuals or groups most likely to value the creation of that benefit. Essentially, there are three types of benefits related to the work of nonprofits:[17]

- *Private* benefits accrue directly to the individual who participates and has limited direct benefit beyond that. Examples of private benefits are attendance at a private school or season tickets to the opera.

- *Group* benefits are those that are associated with an identifiable sub-group of the larger population. Examples of organizations that produce group benefits are after-school programs and food banks.

---

[16] *Financing Nonprofits: Putting Theory into Practice*, Dennis Young, editor (AltaMira Press, 2007).
[17] Ibid.

- *Community* benefits, at least in theory, are those that have the potential to be enjoyed by everyone, regardless of background. Examples of organizations producing community benefits are the public swimming pool and the public library.

- *Trade* benefits, which usually come in the form of corporate sponsorships. In exchange for a financial contribution, the corporation benefits from its exposure as being affiliated with the good work of your organization.

It is tempting, especially for a new nonprofit, to make the case that everyone is better off if, say, low-income children are able to attend summer arts camp. That is, the default mindset of the nonprofit is often the creation of community benefit. To follow the logic of this thinking, you have to make a connection between attending summer camp and a long-term benefit to the community, which will go something like this: summer arts camp nourishes the imagination, which leads to better academic performance, which leads to higher graduation rates, which means more people are more likely to be employed, which leads to less crime...which means you should care.

While everything can be connected given enough dots to play with, the reality is that not everyone is going to care enough about your particular issue to be compelled to write a check to support it. To repeat an earlier admonition, the goal is not to convince everyone they should care, but to identify those who are predisposed to caring. A funding model should reflect this thinking.

For a nonprofit moving from Idea to Startup, it is critical to long-term success that you have a sense of where you think funding is likely to come from. "Writing grants" and "holding events" do not constitute a strategy. Those are tactics. The strategy is inherent in the decisions about who is invited to your events and what you do once you have everyone in the same room together. And, much to the dismay of many grant-seekers, there is no group of hidden foundations just waiting for you to ask them for money. Far more realistic is the scenario of a few foundations in your domain who already receive more requests than they have money to give. To use a familiar analogy, grant writing is not fishing with a net; it is pinpointing areas where the fish are likely to hang out.

In closing this section, I leave you with two more cautions to help deepen your level of strategic thinking about your business model. First, there are no best-kept secrets in town when it comes to nonprofits. And second, if you insist on believing this about your nonprofit, raising awareness is not the answer to your challenge. While there is something to be said for making your presence known, it is fallacious thinking to believe that if more people know about you, the more money you will raise.

The fact is that if the right people know the right things about you, then you have a better chance of raising money. Figuring who those right people are and the right things they need to know about you is the stuff of strategy. In the case of Caring Communities, the business model is built into the program model. That is, the new housing model is built on the ability and willingness of families to pay housing and program fees. For David, the right people are those families looking for alternative housing options for their adult children with developmental disabilities.

Startup Strategic Position

It is important that a nonprofit moving from Idea to Startup be able to articulate the strategic position it aspires to occupy. The advantages of a clear strategic position at the front end will continue to manifest as the organization evolves. Initially, the position statements require a level of clarity that help the organization communicate more effectively with those outside the organization. Further, the aspirant strategic position provides a baseline of assumptions and expectations by which future activities can be assessed.

The organization featured in this section, Caring Communities, was selected to show the centrality of the aspects of relevance, impact, and sustainability at the beginning. Based on its analysis, Caring Communities has identified the following strategic position to capture its intentions:

Program Position *(what you will do, for whom, under what circumstances)*: Caring Communities will provide an alternative to existing housing options for adults with developmental disabilities.

Market Position *(how you will relate to others operating in your domain)*: Caring Communities will work outside of the traditional housing network and work directly with families. Because it will limit itself to housing, Caring Communities will maintain relationships with other providers for day programming and employment services to the residents.

Resource Position *(how you will support the work of the organization)*: Caring Communities will rely on grants and charitable giving to build the first three homes, at which point it is expected that housing and service fees will fund future construction.

Implementation Indicators

The aspirational nature of Startup strategy requires vigilance on all fronts. Even though the intended strategic position of Caring Communities is built on demonstrated demand from families and supported by a viable financial model, there are some key assumptions that will need monitored throughout the Startup stage. Those include:

- Whether the initial interest in the concept expressed by families will convert into actual commitment to participate.

- Whether the program will be able to attract and retain live-in support staff, a key feature of the residential model.

- Whether land will be available and affordable.

- Whether houses can be built within the established budgets for families.

Summary of Startup Strategy

Lifecycle Characteristics: A perceived community need sparks the founding idea or vision; Programs are launched with sweat equity and passion, with little supportive structure or processes.

Strategic Phase: Aspiration

Key Attribute: Clarity

Aspect of Strategy	Key Task	Guiding Questions
Relevance	Substantiate External Demand	1. Are we clear about who will benefit from the work we do? 2. Is there expressed demand from the people who will benefit? 3. Who else is addressing the same issue? What makes us different?
Impact	Clarify the Theory of Change	1. How well do we understand the factors that contribute to the problem we are trying to solve? 2. Which specific factors will we address through our program? 3. How will participants benefit from what we do?
Sustainability	Establish the Business Model	1. Who is likely to value the benefits we produce? 2. How will we garner financial support from those who value the benefits we produce?
Implementation Goals	Anticipate Productivity Level	1. How many units of service do we expect to provide over the course of a program cycle? 2. How many people do we expect to serve over the course of a program cycle?

CHAPTER 2: THE GROWTH STAGE
Adapting to Life on The Ground

Lexi's Dream Factory ("LDF") was built on a simple idea derived from a profound emotional experience of the founder. As a teenager, Lexi befriended a young boy in her neighborhood who had been adopted from Eastern Europe as an infant. Now five years-old, Zach was battling an aggressive form of cancer. Unfortunately, Zach would succumb to the disease within a year. Prior to his death, Zach asked his parents if he could have a puppy, a request his parents were happy to oblige. At the viewing for Zach, Lexi approached the casket holding her young friend and noticed a picture of Zach and his puppy that had been placed in the casket by his parents. What struck Lexi was the look of pure joy on the face of Zach, mere weeks from death, as he hugged his puppy. At that moment, an idea was born.

LDF was established with the founding purpose of providing joy to young children undergoing cancer treatment by presenting them with a one-time gift costing between five-hundred and one-thousand dollars. Lexi was well aware of the existence of other programs serving sick children that are larger in scope and have national brand recognition. Although the scope of her approach was less ambitious, it was profound in its simplicity. Lexi wanted every child undergoing cancer treatment to experience that brief moment of joy that was reflected in that picture of Zach and his puppy.

The startup years for LDF were modest ones. Lexi was still in college, and her mother would lend her spare time to the organization. A few local fundraisers were held, and every dollar that came to the organization went back out in the form of a gift for a child in one of the hospitals within 100 miles of their home. LDF operated in this fashion for the first seven years of its existence, gradually reaching out to other hospitals in the state when they had extra money. And then, it happened.

LDF caught the eye of the CEO of a large corporation in the capital city of Lexi's home state. The corporation has a foundation arm through which it supports charitable involvement of its employees around the country. The company was willing to give LDF what for them would be a transformational gift. "Could you take this program to the west coast for $250,000 a year," Lexi and her mom were asked. Their response was, "…of course."

It is one thing to plan for growth in anticipation of market expansion. The reality for LDF is that it was in the unenviable position of fire/ready/aim. Prior to this offer, the organization had an annual budget of less than $100,000 and was delivering gifts to children in five hospitals, four of them in their home state. Virtually from one week to the next, LDF went from the kitchen table to the office suite, with a budget of almost

$400,000 and a commitment to deliver gifts to hospitals in Northern California.

It wasn't long after the arrival in Northern California that the embers of the Dream Factory fire had blown over to other areas of the west coast. Local newspapers picked up the story of the program, as did regional television stations. With little marketing effort, requests for gifts were now coming in from hospitals, parents, and donors in Seattle, San Diego, and San Francisco. Chicago and New York would soon follow.

How does a small organization with no paid staff, a small budget, and a local presence scale up to have a national presence within three months? LDF found itself thrust into the choppy rapids of a fast-moving growth curve. They needed a Growth stage strategy.

Growth Strategy

As stated in the previous chapter, a strategic plan to move an organization from Idea to Startup is a grand hypothesis. The primary strategic task in the Startup stage is to clarify the basic elements of the idea, including:

- To whom the organization will matter.
- The kind of impact you intend to create.
- How you will secure the resources you need to support your work.

As you go deeper into strategic planning at the Startup stage, there will be implementation goals, which are estimates of the activity volume and the level of participation you expect during one program cycle.

In short, Startup strategy is about what you intend to do. The strength of any particular Startup strategy is a function of two factors: a) the clarity of articulating your intentions; and, b) the soundness of the overall logic that holds the various elements of your intentions together. As used here, soundness means that the various components of the aspirational strategic position are attainable in their own right and are mutually enforcing in their functionality. The ideal strategic position is where the program idea addresses a substantiated demand: you are doing it differently, better, or more conveniently than others providing similar services; and there are people willing to pay you to provide the service.

Planning for Growth has advantages over planning to move from Idea to Startup. The greatest advantages are a) the passing of time and b) the knowledge accrued during that time. The first step in developing a Growth strategy is to review what has happened up until now. In other words, you need to look backward before looking forward. The strategy review process is ideal for this purpose in that it utilizes the expectations, assumptions, and intentions embedded in the Startup strategy as the baseline for the Growth plan. The strategy review is built around three key questions:

1. What were we thinking then?
2. What has happened since?
3. What do we do next?

Embedded in question #2 is a follow-up question: what have we learned from what has happened? It is at this depth of reflection that you are likely to strike strategic oil. Let's look at LDF as an illustration of the strategic planning for an organization moving from Startup to Growth.

Question 1: "What were we thinking then?"

Like many organizations moving from Idea to Startup, the Startup strategy for LDF was more vision than plan. The value of question 1 to Growth planning is that is makes the implicit more explicit. The Idea to Startup strategy for LDF, whether stated or not, was built on the following elements:

Relevance (What problem are you attempting to solve? To whom will this problem matter? How will your activities benefit them?). The relevance of LDF is as close to an a priori assumption as is possible in the nonprofit sector. Much like the adage about explaining art, if you have to convince someone of the value of providing joy to children with cancer, you are probably barking up the wrong tree.

Impact. The theory of change is simple and straightforward: providing a one-time gift (Action) to children undergoing treatment for cancer (Situation) will bring a moment of joy in the midst of isolation (Consequence). Expectations for implementation were equally modest. Beyond the desire to reach more children, LDF was willing to go with the current and do the best with the money it was able to raise.

Sustainability. The plan for maintaining the activities of LDF was simply to live within their means. Because there was no overhead to speak of, there was no pressure to raise any certain amount of money. Lexi would continue to cast a wide net, capturing a large number of relatively small fish (e.g., hog roasts, coin collections, etc.). The number of gifts granted would reflect that year's catch.

Question 2: "What has happened since?"

This question is multi-faceted. From an internal perspective, the question speaks to the productivity of the program. In the case of LDF, the key indicator of productivity is the number of gifts given to children. Because of the ad hoc nature of the program since its launch, there were no rigid expectations for productivity. There is also a qualitative dimension to the question when viewed from the perspective of external conditions. Do we have strong relationships with the hospitals that are not reliant on one individual on the inside? Are we able to fulfill all of the requests we are receiving? Have we attracted new supporters to the cause? In all cases, the answers to the questions are set against the baseline of expectations and assumptions that were in place during Startup.

The most significant development for LDF is the national exposure they have received and the concomitant push from the board of directors to "go national". Though Lexi's dream for the organization was to be able to bring joy to every child, everywhere, it is safe to assume that neither Lexi nor the board of directors saw this much coming at them in such a sudden manner and with this much velocity. Before deciding where it should go next as an organization, LDF took inventory of the lessons it learned since it was founded. The lessons with strategic significance include the following:

- LDF is an easy sell. Virtually everyone who was exposed to the work of the organization felt instantly connected to it. A common question heard over the past few years was, "how do we get you to come to our hospital?"

- The origin story is as compelling as the work of the organization. Much of the media attention given to the organization centered around the story of Lexi and why she founded the organization at the age of sixteen.

- Operational efficiency would be of paramount importance in the ability of the organization to keep up with demand for gifts.

- LDF has the potential to attract national-level sponsorships, as evidenced by the quarter of a million-dollar grant from the corporate foundation.

A Strategy for Managing Growth

The primary theme in the development of a Growth strategy is disciplined adaptation. Adaptation means grooming the second iteration of the founding purpose based on the actual experiences and lessons learned from the Startup phase. Unlike the movement from Idea to Startup, we now have data by which we can assess the grand hypothesis that launched the organization. Discipline comes from the recognition that the desire to respond to increasing demand for service must be balanced against the financial resources and structural capacity that undergird the mission activities of the organization.

The need for discipline at the Growth stage introduces an additional element into the formula for strategy: boundaries.

Boundaries come in a variety of forms, but generally address the following:

- What we will always do.
- What we will never do.
- How we will set priorities.

Despite the conventional wisdom to the contrary, it is reasonable that a nonprofit sometimes will use the words always and never when setting boundaries for a growth strategy. Usually, these definitive terms are invoked when we are dealing with core values or bedrock principles. For example, a community youth center may set a policy that it will never go into homes and intervene in family disputes involving their youth clients. On the other side, a community transportation network may prioritize certain populations such that they will always schedule medical appointments first when determining routes for the day. It is more likely that an organization will establish a set of criteria that will allow them to establish priorities that require more fluidity and flexibility in their implementation. Using this approach, the community transportation provider may set criteria for deciding who gets the available seats once the demand for medical appointments has been met.

Managing Growth

The defining characteristic of the Growth stage in the Lifecycles framework is that demand for service exceeds the current structural capabilities of the organization. Though LDF began modestly, it is becoming increasingly clear that demand for the program is virtually unlimited. Not only are there hundreds of pediatric cancer hospitals in the country, new cases of childhood cancer show no sign of slowing down anytime soon. Coupled with the overwhelming interest from other locations, it is clear that some structure and boundaries are necessary to manage the anticipated growth.

Having validated its relevance, the next step for LDF was to assess the status of its impact. Because of the simplicity of its theory of change, not much discussion was needed. Wishes were being delivered and the feedback from parents of the recipients and the social workers at the hospitals was laudatory. The biggest question facing LDF was not whether it was creating impact. Rather, strategic challenge was to ensure that they would be able to continue to meet demand without sacrificing the quality of the relationships on which they depend.

The Program Model

What was known for sure was that business as usual was not an option for LDF. Simply put, there weren't enough hours in the day for the two-person staff working out of their home to meet the growing demand for gifts. At least for the moment, money wasn't a problem. Helped along by the corporate gift, LDF was able to attract additional funding. No, money wasn't a problem; keeping up with demand was the presenting challenge.

The board and staff identified a number of potential of scenarios under which the organization could maximize its mission impact within the limitations of its structure. In one scenario, LDF could function as the charitable arm of a for-profit corporation. In effect, this would entail building on the relationship it already had with their partnership corporation. A second scenario was fashioned after the federated model, whereby LDF would support franchises that would operate in various cities as independent organizations functioning under the conditions of a franchise agreement.

LDF settled on a hybrid model it believed would address their present capacity limitations. Rather than independent franchises, LDF would establish affiliate sites that would be made up of groups of local volunteers. Each affiliate site would have three major responsibilities. First, they would raise money locally to support the presence of the Dream Factory in their city. Second, they would coordinate the delivery of gifts to hospitals in their city. And third, each site was responsible for recruiting additional volunteers to assist in fundraising efforts.

The Business Model

Up to this point, LDF made general appeals to individuals, foundations, and businesses for funding that is then used to respond to requests from different sites around the country. The more money in, the more gifts out. The new program model described above has the added benefit of having a revised business model built in, at least partially so. To begin, the organization made a few key points of differentiation. First, the home site was differentiated from the affiliate sites.[18] Second, each affiliate site was considered an individual revenue center. The result is a multi-tiered fundraising strategy with the following components:

- Corporate events that raise general operating support to be dispersed to sites at the discretion of the organization.

- Sponsored events by which other businesses hold events and designate the proceeds to LDF.

- Site events by which affiliate sites host events to support the local presence of LDF.

---

[18] The home site is made up of hospitals in three cities in the home state.

Eighty percent of funds raised locally are designated for gifts to children at that site, while twenty percent is returned to the organization. In addition to events, LDF continues to identify and cultivate potential major donors at both the corporate and site levels.

The Growth Strategic Position

Whereas Startup strategy is a grand hypothesis built on intentions and expectations, Growth strategy represents a revised hypothesis built on new information gleaned from experience. Based on the lessons learned over its startup period, LDF will pursue the following strategic position for its Growth stage:

- **Program Position** *(what you will do, for whom, under what circumstances)*: LDF affirms its commitment to providing one-time gifts to children and youth undergoing treatment for cancer.

- **Market Position** *(how you will relate to others operating in your domain)*: LDF seeks to broaden its reach by building a network of affiliate sites in major cities that have a children's oncology hospital or clinic.

- **Resource Position** *(how you will support your work)*: LDF embraces its reliance on charitable funding and will adopt a two-pronged approach. First, it will continue to raise money at the corporate level through events and major donor development. Second, LDF will build the capacity of affiliate sites to raise money locally.

Key Indicators

Confidence should grow as an organization moves from Startup to Growth, but there still remains a degree of uncertainty. With more experience comes more insight, which could lead to more refinement of the strategy. For LDF, the focus over the next one or two years will be on the following questions:

- Is 20% from affiliate site events appropriate to the amount of support required by the sites?

- Can LDF develop affiliate sites while maintaining an acceptable number of gifts given to existing hospitals?

- What is a reasonable expectation for local affiliates to become self-sufficient and self-directed?

Summary of Growth Strategy

Lifecyle Characteristics: Program opportunity and service demand exceed current systems and structural capabilities.

Strategic Phase: Adaptation

Key Attribute: Discipline

Aspect of Strategy	Key Task	Guiding Questions
Relevance	Assess Emergent Demand	1. How strong is demand relative to your expectations? 2. Do you anticipate change in demand moving forward?
Impact	Refine the Program Model	1. Was the program model implemented as planned? 2. Do participants value the program as expected? 3. Are there program elements that aren't having the desired result?
Sustainability	Revise the Business Model	1. Are you attracting the resources you expected and from the sources you expected? 2. Are you able to establish an operating reserve?
Boundaries	Establish Priorities and Limitations	1. Are there demand elements that you are not able to meet? 2. Have you developed priorities in the event demand continues to exceed your capabilities?

CHAPTER 3: THE MATURITY STAGE
Building on The Core

Organizational Resilience

We've all seen the tall, thin inflated characters waving wildly outside of care dealerships and appliance stores. The character has no control over the elements that animate it. Rather, the frequency and intensity of its movements are a function of the direction and speed of the wind. However, the flailing is not the defining characteristic of the character. More significant to its existence is the fact that, though swaying wildly, the character never leaves its spot. It reacts and responds, but its location is fixed. The inflatable character is anchored. It is only because of that anchor that the inflatable character can withstand the unexpected and the disruptive.

Resilience is defined as the capacity to experience massive change while maintaining the integrity of the original.[19] An example of resilience in nature is the re-emergence of new saplings following a wildfire. The destructive effects of the event sow the seeds—literally—of the eventual return of the forest. Like the forest, the survival of a nonprofit may depend on its ability to evolve as the conditions to which it has become accustomed change without warning.

---

[19] Frances Westley, et al, *Getting to Maybe: How the World is Changed* (Vintage Canada, 2006).

Some scholars of organizational development suggest that resilience occurs in stages. Specifically, a resilient organization is one that a) responds to what it has learned from its past, b) takes action to respond to current challenges, and c) anticipates disruptions or major changes that may occur in the future.[20] Regardless of stage, a key enabler of resilience is the ability to recognize patterns while in the midst of them.[21]

Anchoring the Organization

This plight of the inflatable character is an apt metaphor for strategy at the Mature stage. Over its long history, Harvest Home has had its share of shifting winds. The difference this time is that the threat from the latest wind shift is existential. Simply put, Harvest Home will not be able to afford to maintain its mission unless it makes fundamental changes to its program and business model. In other words, Harvest Home must be resilient.

Harvest Home was founded in the late 1800's by a group of churches as a place to send needy children from their home communities. Many were orphans, but some were sent there because families were no longer able to care for them. Once there, the youth were educated and taught how to farm. Some of the children eventually would be adopted while others ended up

[20] Duchek, S. Organizational resilience: a capability-based conceptualization. *Bus Res* **13,** 215–246 (2020). https://doi.org/10.1007/s40685-019-0085-7
[21] Westley, et al.

with foster families. In addition to being the source of referrals, the group of churches were the major source of funding for Harvest Home.

Over time, the residents at Harvest Home would change in response to the changing social norms and family conditions. In addition to orphans, Harvest Home would become a surrogate home for unwed mothers and later to a broad category of "wayward youth" – mostly boys. But the adoptions continued, in addition to the education of the young women. Churches continued to be the primary funding source during this period.

The 1970's was a defining period for Harvest Home. It was during this time that state governments assumed a prominent role in ensuring child welfare and protection by providing residential placements for children and youth in need of intensive mental and behavioral health treatment. Children and youth now were sent to Harvest Home by judges, schools, and child protective services. Much like with the churches in its early years, Harvest Home depended on these various referring entities for clients and the funding to support them.

From that point forward, Harvest Home would be tightly linked to the systems of children and youth support directed and funded by a group of government entities. There have been some modifications to the treatment modalities over the years, but the strategic position of Harvest Home was firmly grounded in the soil of state-funded care for children and youth. Today, government funding makes up almost 90% of total revenues for Harvest Home.

Beginning in the late 2000's, the state child welfare system began a consistent and continuous movement away from residential placements in favor of outpatient and community-based services. This is either good news or devastating news, depending on the lens through which you view it. On the one hand, more children are receiving services through Harvest Home because of the availability of non-residential services. On the other hand, the loss of reimbursement for 24/7 care makes it difficult for Harvest Home to maintain the rather large physical plant built around its residential program.

With the shift in the state's priorities toward non-residential services, Harvest Home was facing a major disruption that threatened to destroy the very foundation on which the organization had operated for the past forty years. The ten-year trends on client placements and revenue from the state spoke loudly. If Harvest Home didn't realign its program and business models, it would be a slow and steady bleed of surplus revenues.

For a Mature organization, being resilient requires that the organization be anchored, just like the inflatable character. This entails looking backward in search of the patterns that reveal the persistent characteristics that have endured through past disruptions and challenges. We will refer to these enduring characteristics collectively as the organizational core. The organizational core is revealed through the distillation of the organizational history down to responses to these three questions:

1. Who needs you most?
2. What do they need most from you?
3. What are your defining qualities?

At first glance, it may appear that the shifts from orphans, to unwed mothers, and eventually to referrals from the State child welfare system signify for Harvest Home changes in strategy at best and mission drift at worst. Either way, it may appear that the organization was not anchored. However, a deeper reflection on the question of 'who needs you most' reveals a meaningful pattern. While the circumstances that brought youth to Harvest Home changed over time, what remained constant is that these groups of youth represented the neediest at a particular time in history. Thus, the question 1 answered: who needs us most are those youth in the most difficult of social circumstances.[22]

The same process of high-level reflection led to a clear answer to the second question. The orphans worked the farm; the unwed mothers were provided pre-natal care and adoptions were arranged for their newborn babies; youth referred by the child welfare system attend school, participate in recreational activities, and receive intensive therapy. It would be easy to

---

[22] This statement implies that the difficult circumstances of the youth are within the scope of the mission.

conclude that what those youth needed most from Harvest Home was to be removed from their current environment. That is part of it, for sure. By digging deeper, the organization realized that the residential aspect of the program was but a means to an end. The residential experience allowed Harvest Home to provide the youth with what they needed most: structure, continuity of relationships, and intensive therapeutic interventions.

Asking a nonprofit to answer question 3 can be a bit like asking the fish to describe the water. Defining qualities often are embedded in the intangible characteristics of the organization: its values, its treatment philosophies, even the nature of the relationships with its clients. While Harvest Home was able to articulate each of these intangible characteristics for itself, its defining quality was found in a tagline it had adopted a few decades earlier: creating a better future for children...whatever it takes. Harvest Home had identified a pattern of accepting clients that had not succeeded anywhere else or who would not be taken in by anyone else. Once they accepted a client, Harvest Home would improvise to meet the unique, often difficult needs of that client. Doing whatever it takes wasn't just a slogan. It was in the water.

I have written elsewhere about the importance of deep reflection in the formulation of the organizational core.[23] Put simply, lack of clarity and focus in the formulation of the core

---

[23] Stone, M.E. (2017). *Strategy from the Inside Out: A Nonprofit's Guide to Meaningful Strategy.* Self-Published.

will show up later in the strategy development process. Harvest Home did not arrive at its definition of the organizational in one facilitated session with a flip chart and sticky notes. It was driven by the questions, which drove the organization to delve into its history with the aid of data revealing trends and patterns, which often led to more questions. In short, there is no shortcut that will lead to the definition of the organizational core. It is the heavy lifting in the development of strategy for a Mature organization.

With the organization firmly anchored in the elements of its organizational core, Harvest Home began looking forward.

Relevance

Generally speaking, the question regarding the relevance of Harvest Home is this: Is there still demand for an organization that will do whatever it takes to provide structure, continuity of relationships, and intensive interventions for those youth in the most difficult social circumstances? To substantiate its response, Harvest Home must take a finer-grained look at its relevance by revisiting the questions that would have been posed at the Startup stage. Those questions are:

- Are we clear about who will benefit from the work we do?
- Is there expressed demand from the people who will benefit?
- Who else is addressing the same issue? What makes us different?

The answer to the first question for Harvest Home is embedded in its definition of its organizational core. The answer to the second question is equally apparent when you recall the nature of the relationship between benefit and demand. Demand is a function of the degree to which people outside your organization value the type of benefit you create (i.e., private, group, community, or public). Remembering that 'who cares is who pays', it is clear that the demand for the services of Harvest Home is still there, as expressed by the willingness of government entities to support the work. This is the prototypical model of a public benefit organization.

It is when we arrive at question 3 that the strategic stakes get higher for Harvest Home. Since the 1970's, Harvest Home has been positioned as one provider in a statewide network of organizations serving youth with behavioral and emotional challenges. Though the other providers in the network were competitors per se (because consumers have other options), in reality there were enough funding and referrals from the various government agencies to keep the beds full at most places. That was, until the great retraction started in the early 2000's.

Not only did the state shift its funding to non-residential services for youth, there was speculation that the grand design was to remove excess capacity to the point that only a handful of larger providers would be left standing. This was both encouraging and daunting for Harvest Home. On the one hand, it had been around long enough to establish a strong reputation among the various government agencies. On the other hand, the treatment and reimbursement schedules offered by the state would not keep Harvest Home above water financially.

The strategic challenge for Harvest Home was now clear: how can it, working from its organizational core, position itself so that it emerges as one of the survivors in a retracting market?

Impact

There are numerous criteria by which a nonprofit can make program decisions. I have seen core programs cut because they were money-losers, while marginally-relevant programs were kept out of a sense of nostalgia. Let's be clear about one thing: there are no easy decisions when it comes to cutting programs or expenses. However, some approaches are better than others. Strictly speaking, program and resource decisions should be made in consideration of the relative strategic value to the organization. The ability to make strategic decisions in this manner rests on the ability of the organization to properly manage the trade-offs.

In its simplest form, relative strategic value is two-dimensional. I recommend beginning with a process I call core mapping. To begin, draw a set of three concentric circles. Next, review the elements of the organizational core. Finally, place each program within one of the three concentric circles based on the extent to which it aligns with the three elements of the organizational core. Those programs that address all three are placed in the center circle; those that deviate from the core in one of the three aspects of the core are placed in the second circle. If any program deviates from more than one aspect of the organizational core are placed in the outer circle. Below is a simplified version of the core mapping of Harvest Home programs.

Figure 4: Core Mapping of Harvest Home Programs

Youth Services

Family Counseling

Community Counseling

Youth services, quite literally, have formed the core of Harvest Home from the time of its founding. Family counseling is in the second ring because it deviates from the core definition of "who needs you most". Even though the counseling takes place on the Harvest Home campus, it is not placed in the center circle because it does not have an exclusive focus on youth.[24]

---

[24] While family counseling involves youth, the program is open to families who do not have youth who are receiving other services from Harvest Home. If this sounds like splitting hairs, then you understand the importance of conceptual precision in this process. Its consequences will become apparent as the process continues.

Finally, community counseling is placed in the outer circle because it does not have an exclusive focus on youth; and it addresses a wide range of psycho-social issues, such as substance abuse and adult domestic relationships.

Now that the programs have been sorted based on their adherence to the elements of the organizational core, it is time to introduce the second dimension of strategic value: profitability.[25] It is at this point that the trade-offs become obvious. Through the exercise, Harvest Home discovered the following:

- Youth services, because of the decrease in reimbursement from the state, will require an internal subsidy to sustain.[26] The one exception is the Secured program, which is for youth at risk of harm to themselves or others. This program is residential, fully reimbursable, and remains a priority for the state.

- Family counseling, though not considered core, is budget neutral. The ancillary benefit of the program is that it introduces families to Harvest Home, who

---

[25] I use the term "profitability" generally to include cost versus revenue, in addition to the hidden costs. Those include the difficulty of generating the revenue for the program and the reliability of the funding source.

[26] Internal subsidy is any unrestricted funding that is allocated by the organization. The source of the funding (i.e., unrestricted grants, charitable giving, investment earnings, or operating reserves) is irrelevant.

may seek out additional services for their youth at a later time.

- Community counseling was launched as a way to utilize the therapeutic expertise of Harvest Home to generate additional revenue that could be used to subsidize its youth services. After two years of operation, the center has yet to produce any surplus revenue.

Sustainability

The sustainability of any nonprofit begins with the basics of profit and loss. Most nonprofits will have a mix of money-makers and money-losers scattered across the core map. The goal is not to achieve mission purity by eliminating everything outside of the center circle; nor is it always advisable to grow core programs. To reiterate, strategy is about achieving the appropriate balance through the intentional management of trade-offs. How much are you willing to move outside of your center circle in order to generate surplus revenue? At what point do those second and third ring activities begin to diminish your ability to create impact in your inner circle programs? While there is no universal standard for making these decisions, there are decisions that are right for each individual organization.

One thing was clear. If Harvest Home were to continue to operate as it had over the past 40 years, it would be akin to following the Pied Piper over the cliff. The reimbursements coming from the various state agencies simply did not keep pace with the cost of maintaining the physical infrastructure that Harvest Home had built up over those forty years. The financial ground under Harvest Home had shifted to the point where business as usual could no longer be afforded.

Affirming the Strategic Position

Resilience has been defined as the ability to let go and hang on simultaneously.[27] In the vernacular of strategy, I refer to the resiliency approach to strategy as "affirm and tweak". What is affirmed are the core elements of your organization as they have become embedded over time. What is tweaked in a Mature strategy is the programmatic expression of that core. Said another way, you let go of the things that get in the way of you being a better version of who you are as an organization.

In the end, Harvest Home affirmed the components of its strategic position in their present form and, in recognition of the changes in its external environment, made programmatic tweaks that they believe will lead to even greater relevance, impact, and sustainability. The elements of the Harvest Home strategic position are presented below.

---

[27] Westley, et al, page 71.

Program Position *(what you will do, for whom, under what circumstances)*: Harvest Home will continue to provide comprehensive services, rooted in intensive therapy, for youth facing the most difficult social circumstances. In recognition of the changing priorities at the state level, Harvest Home make the following adjustments to its program model:

- Reduce by roughly two-thirds the number of beds it would hold for noncritical residential referrals from state agencies.

- Double its capacity to receive referrals to the Secure program, which was profitable and produced outcomes that exceeded the state average.[28]

- Expand its capacity to serve families and youth through its non-residential counseling programs.

Market Position *(how you will relate to others operating in your domain)*: Harvest Home will maintain its status as a youth service provider for the state department of child welfare. Simultaneously, it will

---

[28] Harvest Home worked under a statewide outcomes program, which was used to determine funding levels.

present its services more directly to the general public rather than interfacing only with referring agencies. To this end, Harvest Home will:

- Seek independent accreditation for the on-site school and offer enrollment to the community-at-large.

- Sever its contractual relationship to serve as an alternative school for students referred by local public-school system.

Resource Position *(how you will support the work of the organization)*: It is likely that Harvest will always be dependent of government agencies as its primary source of revenue. Given the shift to lower-cost options by the state, Harvest Home will seek to generate more fee-for-service revenues through its expanded programs.

Key Indicators

For a Mature organization, managing profit and loss is only one piece of a sustainable resource position. The key to long-term sustainability is the preservation of the durable assets of the organization, such as investment funds, operating reserves, and capital improvement funds. How those assets are utilized, however, depends on the strategic positioning of the organization.

On the heels of the strategic development process, Harvest Home underwent preparation for a multi-year capital campaign that would allow it to update and rescale its campus to align with the strategic position. Moving forward, Harvest Home will monitor the following activities for signs of progress:

- The success of capital campaign.
- The ability to attract students directly to the on-site school.
- The potential for the community counseling centers to become a profit center.

In launching of its capital campaign, Harvest Home described itself as "not what we used to be but still who we've always been". Its ability to affirm and tweak captures the very essence of organizational resilience: hang on the best of who you are while letting go of the things that prevent the best expression of who you are.

Summary of Maturity Strategy

Lifecyle Characteristics: The nonprofit has a reputation for providing steady, relevant and vital services to the community and operates with a solid organizational foundation and overall sense of security.

Strategic Phase: Affirmation

Key Attribute: Resilience

Aspect of Strategy	Key Task	Guiding Questions
Relevance	Identify Essential Characteristics	1. In which program areas do you occupy a niche or are considered a market leader? 2. What are the core competencies of the organization?
Impact	Assess Strategic Value of Programs	1. In what areas of service are you able to demonstrate the greatest impact among your target population? 2. Are there additional needs among your target population that you can address? 3. Are there other populations who can benefit from your current programs and core competencies?
Sustainability	Preserve Long-term Assets	1. Are we prepared for capital improvements? 2. Do we have a strategy for the use of earnings from investments? 3. Are we prepared for unexpected changes in leadership or funding?
Organizational Core		1. Historically, who has benefitted most from what you do? 2. Specially, what are the demonstrated benefits for that group? 3. What are the enduring characteristics of your organization?

CHAPTER 4: THE TURNAROUND STAGE
Is There Anything Worth Fighting For?

Readers familiar with the Lifecycle Stages framework will notice that I skipped over the stage between Mature and Turnaround. That missing stage, for those not familiar with the framework, is the Decline stage. According the Lifecycle Stages framework, organizations in Decline exhibit three interrelated characteristics. First, they make safe decisions based on internal factors rather than client needs. Second, and as a consequence of the first, client census diminishes to the point that the third characteristic appears: insufficient income to cover operating expenses.[29]

Organizations in Decline are a bit like a traffic accident you drive past after the fact. It is obvious what has happened— two cars collided. What may not be obvious is how and why it happened. From the perspective of strategic positioning, the why and how an organization gets to the Decline stage can be distilled down to two potential scenarios. Decline is what happs when a Mature organization either a) loses sight of who it is, or b) becomes complacent with who it is.[30]

An example of the first scenario is the nonprofit that broadens the scope of its programs to the point that the

---

[29] Kenney Stevens, *Nonprofit Lifecycles.*
[30] It is possible for a nonprofit to go into Decline without ever reaching Maturity. Startups fail and nonprofits in the Growth phase never find equilibrium. For purposes of this chapter, I am focusing exclusively on Mature organizations that go into Decline and how they respond.

organization buckles under its own weight. The vernacular for this phenomenon is "chasing money" and the effect is a perpetual struggle to replace grant funding in order to maintain programs and the staff that run them. Even if the organization is able to continue, it is usually at the expense of mission impact and staff sanity.

In this chapter, I will focus on the second scenario: nonprofits who attained a certain level of relevance, impact, and sustainability and then became complacent. Stated plainly, these organizations get caught standing flat-footed while the rest of the world slowly, quietly, and steadily passed them by. This chapter will describe the plight of one nonprofit that found itself in Decline and how it explored various Turnaround scenarios.

From Maturity to Decline

Senior Services of Anderson County ("SSAC") was founded on the heels of the 1974 Older Americans Act. Like its counterparts around the state and around the country, SSAC received funding through the Act to provide services to senior citizens. The services ranged from transportation to the wide variety of in-home services. SSAC went through several iterations over the years, each one in response to new service opportunities funded through the Older Americans Act. Things appeared to be going smoothly for SSAC.

Beginning in the early 2000's, the world around SSAC began to change. SSAC either did not notice the changes or did not understand how the changes would affect them. While they were busy maintaining the status quo, the number of specialized services in the area had been expanding, resulting in the steady decline in the number of clients seeking their services. Whereas SSAC once was the sole provider of senior transportation, there were now numerous private companies competing for market share. And whereas they were the first to provide in-home services, numerous providers had developed niches in focused areas such as home repairs, in-home nursing, and meal delivery. Simply put, the unique market position SSAC enjoyed over the years had all but evaporated.

Strategy development for a Mature organization is approached from a position of strength. They move forward by building on the competencies and momentum developed over their history. By contrast, nonprofits in Decline are starting from a position of frailty at best, weakness at worst. In effect, a Turnaround strategy is like starting over.[31] If SSAC were to move forward, they must avoid the mistakes of their past. Being in Decline, the questions faced by SSAC are these:

- Are we still relevant? If not, what would it take to re-establish relevancy?

- Are we creating unique impact? If not, where can we create a niche for ourselves?

---

[31] The Lifecycle Stages framework shows the path from Turnaround leads back to the region between Startup and Growth.

- Can we find the funding to support our programs?

Repositioning the organization will take a lot of effort and a lot of time to accomplish. If the answer to any one of the three questions above is 'no', the challenge facing the organization is daunting. The common metaphor for this situation is turning the Titanic. Perhaps a more apt metaphor is this: repositioning a nonprofit in Decline is akin to building a whole new ship, retraining the crew, and then hoping you can sell enough tickets to the places you think people want to go. It is this realization that prompts the question that often is left unspoken: is there anything left worth fighting for?

Relevance

Is SSAC still relevant? To answer this, let's return to the criteria for relevance at the Startup stage. Establishing relevance is a matter of substantiating demand from people outside the organization, including the intended beneficiaries and the people who value the benefits you provide such that are willing to pay you to deliver the services. The basis of relevance is found in the following three questions:

- What problem are you attempting to solve?
- To whom will this problem matter?
- How will your activities benefit them?

SSAC continues to solve the problem that brought it into existence, which is the isolation and lack of mobility of senior citizens. This matters to the senior citizens, but also to the families of seniors who are concerned with the quality of life of their parents. In addition, funding is still available through various government agencies and local foundations. It is clear that, despite its own internal challenges, the founding purpose of SSAC remains relevant.

Impact

The underlying assumptions and expectations about how SSAC would approach the problem of isolation and immobility of senior citizens (the logic) and the intended benefits for participants (the outcomes) are as valid today as they were at the time of its founding. Said another way, they appear to be doing the right things for the right people. The first sign—or would-be sign—of impending trouble for SSAC is the decrease in the type and number of services and participants (the Implementation). Even so, the clients that were being served by SSAC were getting the services they expected with no reason to suspect any dissatisfaction.

Sustainability

At last, we come to the money question. Given that a) the mission of SSAC remains relevant, and b) the services they provide are benefitting clients, what would it take to make SSAC sustainable? An analysis of the current financial standing of SSAC revealed a few major liabilities. First, the senior transportation program, its largest source of revenue, costs more to run than the revenue it generates. Second, as the demand for in-home services become more specialized (e.g., medical care, mental health services), SSAC was able to provide the most basic and least reimbursable types of services.

SSAC faced three options. First, they could reposition themselves in light of the new circumstances. Second, they could go out of business. And third, they could pursue some type of merger arrangement with a larger service provider. Since the focus of this chapter is Turnaround strategy, I will retrace the steps taken by SSAC to decide whether it would be able to develop a path for itself moving forward.

Repositioning

The three tasks involved in the repositioning are these:

- Realign mission priorities.
- Narrow the scope of impact.
- Reestablish a business model.

Let's consider these options in the context of the elements of the strategic position.

- To establish a program position (what you will do, for whom, under what circumstances), SSAC could either a) retool and compete for market share in its historic areas of service, or b) find an available niche and reposition itself as a specialist in one of the industry's areas of demand.

- A viable market position (how you will relate to others in your domain) for SSAC is dependent upon the program position it chooses. If it chose to remain a comprehensive provider, SSAC would need to differentiate itself in some meaningful way from the range of specialty providers operating currently. Even in choosing a niche, SSAC would have to build the strength, capacity, and reputation to be seen as the 'best in class' in that particular line of service.

- As the tail that wags the dog, the resource position (how you will support your work) is the final arbiter of the viability of the strategic position. For SSAC to reposition, it would need to move away from its primary dependence on government contracts and local foundation grants, and develop its programs based on a fee-for-service model. SSAC has learned from its history that the ability to raise charitable dollars is hampered because of the perception that its services provide a private benefit. For the average person, the hesitation is giving to an organization that is providing services that a family should provide.

Turnaround or Terminate?

Clearly, much had changed in the operating domain of SSAC. New competitors, new areas of need, and new types of services have all come onto the scene in the past decade. All the while, SSAC kept its focus internally, viewing declining revenue as a fundraising challenge and a need for operational efficiency. In reality, their financial challenges were early indications of a shrinking market niche. SSAC now understands that it will require a great deal of energy, drive, and stamina to keep running, with no assurance that it will ever finish the race.

SSAC was clear on two things. First, their work still mattered to the people they serve. They remain relevant. Mission relevance is the first hurdle to clear for a nonprofit in Decline. If what you do no longer matters to anyone outside your organization, then...well, nothing else matters. But confirming relevance is far from crossing the finish line. The next set of questions will give SSAC a better sense of just how long the race will be:

- What significant changes have occurred in our domain of operation?
- Are there new competitors?
- Have the needs of our clientele changed?

These questions made clear the second aspect of its circumstances. Even with a niche strategy, SSAC faced a long road ahead in reaching financial equilibrium. The main challenge was how to disengage from the high cost programs that were highly competitive (e.g., transportation) while establishing itself as a high-quality provider in areas of specialization. In the end, SSAC decided it could best serve seniors and the broader system of senior care by maintaining its existing in-home care services and operating under the banner of a larger 501(c)(3) organization. For SSAC, its best hope of continuing its founding mission was to place in a larger programmatic and organizational context.

Summary of Turnaround Strategy

Lifecyle Characteristics: The organization is at a critical juncture because of lost market share and revenues but is taking decisive action to reverse prior actions in favor or market relevance and organizational viability.

Strategic Phase: Repositioning

Key Attribute: Focus

Aspect of Strategy	Key Task	Guiding Questions

Relevance	Realign Mission Priorities	1. What significant changes have occurred in your domain of operation?
		  a. Are there new competitors?
		  b. Have the needs of your clientele changed?

Impact	Narrow the Scope of Impact	1. What are the trends in the number of people served? 2. How well do you understand why people choose your services?
Sustainability	Reestablish a Business Model	1. How long can you continue to operate under the current conditions? 2. Are there scenarios under which you can become profitable?
Organizational Core	Eliminate Marginal Activities	1. Historically, who has benefitted most from what you do? 2. Specially, what are the demonstrated benefits for that group? 3. Can you create a viable strategic position serving only this group?

CHAPTER 5: STRATEGY EXECUTION:
Bridging Vision and Action

In the image of capacity-building presented in the Introduction, the tabletop (programs) supports the vase (mission). The table legs represent the foundational strength necessary to support the nonprofit in the areas of management, governance, resources, and systems. Strategic positioning, in this scenario, can be thought of as ensuring the stability of the vase and deciding where the table should be placed. Figure 5 below illustrates the relationship between mission, strategy, and programs.

Figure 5: Strategic Positioning and Capacity-Building

As Thomas McLaughlin points out, strategic positioning consists of two parts: deciding where to go, then planning how to get there.[32] It has become a truism of organizational life that it is much easier to develop a strategic plan than it is to execute one. For a number of reasons, organizations stumble when moving from the first part of strategy to the second part. It is my belief that the inability to execute a strategy is the result of a fundamental flaw in strategic planning: the failure to create a strategic plan that is executable.

I have argued that strategy is a term that has become inherently ambiguous by its use as a stand-in word for a lot of different types and levels of activity. In the most general sense, strategy can be understood as the exercise of intentional choice regarding the use of organizational resources. As we move from vision to action, I recommend we sharpen our language about strategy to encompass two levels of activity:

Macro-Level Strategy: This is big-picture/long-term thinking that is concerned with the positioning of the organization such that it is able to create the greatest mission impact in the most sustainable manner. Macro-level strategy is built around a small number of questions that by now should be familiar to you:

---

[32] Thomas McLaughlin, *Nonprofit Strategic Planning: Decide Where to Be, Plan What to Do* (Wiley 2006).

- What will we do, for whom, to what end?
- How do we differentiate from others in our domain?
- What is the most reliable funding mix, given the nature of our work?

Micro-Level Strategy: Whereas macro-level strategy is about positioning, micro-level strategy is about implementation. The vantage point for micro-level strategy is one that provides a clear line of sight to the daily operational and program decisions and activities that will move the organization in the direction it has chosen for itself. Micro-level strategy is built around a small number of more short-term and intermediate tasks, such as:

- Setting priorities for the use of staff time.
- Adapting programs to the changing needs of clients.
- Making connections with others operating within your domain.

One requirement of successful strategy execution is the ability to differentiate between the two levels of strategy. Figure 6 shows the movement from macro-level strategy (which is long-term and aimed at movement); to micro-level strategy, which is short-term and focused on activities). As we work down the pyramid from planning to implementation, we encounter a key transition point in the form of strategic priorities.

Figure 6: Differentiating Levels of Strategy

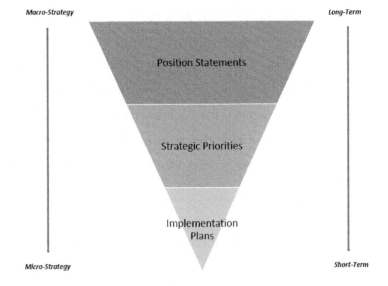

Strategic Priorities

In the preceding chapters we focused on the top of the pyramid by viewing approaching strategic positioning based on the Lifecycle Stage of the nonprofit. With enough coaching and guidance, a nonprofit can articulate its desired strategic position, whether they use this exact vocabulary or not. At the other end, managers are good at making action plans. However, in the words of McLaughlin, "the typical strategic plan has turned into a hopelessly complex and unachievable collection of small ideas leading nowhere in particular."[33] Harsh words, but spot on. Planning becomes strategic only when the top and bottom of the pyramid are aligned. The lynchpin of that alignment are the strategic priorities.

Strategic priorities are defined as the key opportunities and challenges that affect your ability to attain, maintain, or enhance the desired strategic position. Think of strategic priorities as akin to putting horses in the starting gate prior to the start of the race. As you move from vision to action, you want to make sure that everyone knows where the organization is trying to go and what it will take to get there. Strategic priorities, like the starting gate, ensure that everyone in the organization is lined up and facing the same way. Quality strategic priorities have the following characteristics:

- They are directional and action-oriented (increase, expand, etc.)
- Though general in direction, they lead to specificity in implementation.
- They cut across all or most areas of the organization.

---

[33] Page 7

Below is an example of a quality strategic priority in the context of the strategy pyramid.

Position Statement (Resource): To attain greater financial stability in the long-term, we must lessen our vulnerability to shifts in government funding.

Strategic Priority: We will grow our operating endowment to secure long-term operations.

Implementation Plan: We will develop and launch a capital campaign aimed at major gifts for the operating endowment.

We can expect that the development and launch of a capital campaign will involve a number of people operating in a variety of roles. While each participant may run a slightly different course in reaching the goal, the important thing is that everyone knows from the start where the finish line is.

The starting gate is not designed to be an instrument of constraint. Rather, think of it as a management tool, an imposed discipline to prevent chaos on the racetrack. Likewise, without a way to define and organize strategic priorities, well-intentioned staff and board members run the risk of drifting across several lanes of traffic and disrupting the progress of the entire field. (I believe I have now pressed all of the oil out of the horse race metaphor.) To prevent strategic chaos, a management tool for strategy execution is needed.

The elements of the capacity-building model—program, management, governance, resources, and systems—provide a useful and durable starting gate for strategic activities. To this list of elements, I add one other: external relations. Taken together, these six areas represent the major levers that can be manipulated by a nonprofit to move toward the strategic destination it has chosen for itself.

Tables 4, 5, 6, and 7 at the end of this section show the process by which strategic positioning is translated into strategic priorities. Each table represents one of the four case study organizations, each at a different Lifecycle Stage. The tables include the following categories:

- The broad capacity outcome for each of the six areas based on the Lifecycle Stage of the organization.[34]

- The strategic considerations based on the strategic phase that is aligned with the Lifecycle Stage.

---

[34] Descriptions taken from Nonprofit Lifecycles, with the exception of *external relations*.

- The strategic priorities that will guide the work of the organization over the next two to three years.

There is one qualifier in use of the capacity-building model for identifying and organizing strategic priorities. While capacity-building is important, regardless of the desired strategic position, not all capacity-building needs necessarily have strategic significance. For example, it is important for any nonprofit to upgrade its internal systems as needed. However, "upgrading internal systems" takes on strategic significance if you are ramping up to take on a new line of service that has stringent data management requirements. The lesson: do not conflate the important with the strategic.

Table 3: Strategic Priorities for **Caring Communities**

	Capacity Outcomes (Idea to Startup Stage)	Strategic Considerations (Aspirations Phase)	Strategic Priorities
Program	Services delivered as planned; meeting client expectations.	Clarify the program model based on external demand and available resources.	Institute policies and procedures for selecting families.
Management	Shift from volunteers to paid staff with clear roles and responsibilities.	Clarify the role(s) to be played by the founder or founding CEO.	Build a staffing model founded on the Founder's background in direct service delivery.
Governance	Shift from individuals with connection to the mission or founder, to those outside the "inner circle".	Balance business oversight with the need for specific content expertise.	Recruit board members with expertise in finance, building codes, and zoning.
Resources	Shift from sweat equity to outside funding.	Determine the type and amount of needed for startup activities.	Secure major gifts to fund the first three group homes.
Systems	Shift from in-kind support to outsourced services.	Build systems that can manage anticipated growth.	Secure a data management system capable of managing processes and tracking multiple mortgages.
External Relations	Awareness of organization among key external parties.	Determine who needs to know about you, what you want them to know, and what you need them to do.	Develop vehicles to keep prospective families updated and involved.

Table 4: Strategic Priorities for **Lexi's Dream Factory**

	Capacity Outcomes (Growth Stage)	Strategic Considerations (Adaptation Phase)	Strategic Priorities
Programs	Distinctive programming; uniformity in program delivery	Adapt the program model to meet demand within capacity limitations.	Develop criteria and supporting materials for affiliate sites.
Management	Formalized job descriptions; set of consensual organizational priorities.	Determine the desired mix of internal versus external responsibilities for the CEO.	Adjust the staffing model to reflect the need for the CEO to spend time on affiliate site development.
Governance	Shared board/staff ownership; board structures and processes established.	Determine the desired mix of governance, operations, advisory, and resource development.	Set expectations for board members regarding securing corporate sponsorships and major donors.
Resources	Desirable revenue mix; understanding of cost of doing business.	Calculate the relative "cost of capture" for each revenue type.	Develop two signature events, major donors, supported with short-term "pop-up" events.
Systems	Internal systems updated and professionalized.	Assess the capabilities of the organization relative to internal and external reporting.	Outsource accounting and payroll to free up time for the CEO; Utilize volunteers to expedite gift deliveries.
External Relations	Opportunities in place for the engagement of donors and supporters.	Develop a structure for the use of volunteers.	Create an auxiliary group to assist with events and other fundraising activities.

Table 5: Strategic Priorities for **Harvest Home**

	Capacity Outcomes (Mature Stage)	Strategic Considerations (Affirmation Phase)	Strategic Priorities
Programs	Comprehensive mix of programs; competitive advantages established	Determine the strategic value of each program; build on organizational strengths.	Launch independent school; Increase capacity for Secure referrals.
Management	CEO is active in field development and public policy.	Determine the leadership and management skills needed to move the organization forward.	Involve the CEO in the solicitation of major and capital gifts.
Governance	Board is policy-focused; highly functioning structures and processes.	Ensure leadership succession at the executive and board levels.	Prepare a 3-5-year transition plan in anticipation of the retirement of the current CEO.
Resources	Stable income; access to working capital.	Secure the assets needed to strengthen the organization's strategic position.	Conduct a feasibility study regarding a capital campaign to refurbish and adapt campus buildings.
Systems	Written policies, handbooks, and annual reports are produced and maintained.	Ensure ongoing compliance with external mandates and prohibitions.	Create a Compliance Coordinator position to report directly to the CEO.
External Relations	Investments from key external stakeholders.	Segment donor base by history of support to the organization.	Develop planning giving program for church-related constituents.

Table 6: Strategic Priorities for **SSAC**

	Capacity Outcomes (Decline to Turnaround Stage)	Strategic Considerations (Repositioning Phase)	Strategic Priorities
Program	Fewer programs remain for market and mission relevance.	Determine where unmet demand exists within the broader market.	Identify competitors and collaborators introduced with the new program position.
Management	Streamlined personnel and administrative structures.	Determine the type of organizational arrangement that is most viable (e.g., merger, collaborative, etc.).	Conduct operational audit to determine core capabilities.
Governance	Small but highly committed individuals work to restore credibility, support turnaround efforts of the CEO.	Ensure that a diversity of perspectives is taken into account in the creation of the turnaround plan.	Minimize the number of direct stakeholders (i.e., families of clients, direct service providers) involved in the planning process.
Resources	Payment plans developed to correspond with expected cash flow.	Protect most valuable staff, program, and financial assets first.	Be willing to terminate legacy services that do not add strategic value.
Systems	Policies and procedures streamlined.	Preserve adherence to external mandates and limitations.	Research the implications of a merger on current government service contracts.
External Relations	Organizational credibility reestablished in the community.	Focus on those parties that you depend on most for a successful turnaround.	Initiate discussions with potential partner organizations.

The Strategic Framework

We have a default image of what a strategic plan should look like. I have seen many strategic plans that looked "good" in that the contents were well-organized, the goals were specific, the timelines were tight, and the responsible parties for each objective were identified. However, the plans failed in the area that matter most when it comes to strategy, which is the answer to this question: if/when you complete everything in the plan, how will your organization be more relevant, impactful, or sustainable?

The value of any given strategic plan is in its utility, which depends in part on the quality of the finished product. To this end, I recommend replacing the all-inclusive strategic plan with a concise strategic framework. The difference between the traditional strategic plan and the strategic framework is akin to the difference between a users' manual and a short literary story. A users' manual is written as a step-by-step guide to completing a finite task. Every piece is provided, and the instructions are fool-proof.

In contrast, the strategic framework is not a how-to document. A well-developed strategic framework will have a narrative arc that conveys to the reader how the organization got to where it is, what it has learned about itself and the people it serves, and where it needs to go to remain relevant, impactful, and sustainable.

The ideal strategic framework has the following characteristics:

It is relatively short. Short means the size of the document itself, about three to five pages. This is not a plan with concrete steps but an outline that provides the context and the boundaries from which various actions plans will flow.

It has narrative flow and cohesion. We make meaning of things, as individuals and as organizations, by placing them in the context of a larger arc of experience. The strategic framework should reflect the organizational journey such that someone new to the organization can read it and understand where the organization has been, what it has learned about itself, and where it seeks to go next.

It is not time-dependent. There is no ticking clock when it comes to strategic positioning. Even if there were, organizations never stop trying to create greater mission impact. This is not to say that goals are not an important aspect of planning. Plans have deadlines, strategic positions do not.

In short, the strategic framework is a guide for long-term planning and ongoing decisions. It is not a blueprint for immediate action. Like any good heuristic tool, the strategic framework relies on a stable structure to tell the story of the organization. Specifically, the strategic framework contains the following elements:

- A brief strategic history of the organization, focusing on major milestones and significant shifts.

- A definition of the organizational core, which encompasses the following:
    - Who has benefitted most from what you do?

    - What are the demonstrated benefits for that group?

    - What are the enduring characteristics of your organization?

- A description of the desired strategic position, which encompasses:
    - What you will do, for whom, and to what end (Program Position).

    - How you will relate to and differentiate yourself from others in your domain (Market Position).

- How you will support the work of the organization (Resource Position).

• A manageable list of strategic priorities that will guide the work of the organization in the short- to intermediate-term.

It is at this point that the strategy development process has transitioned from vision to action. While a variety of implementation plans may be needed to support a specific strategic priority, the priority itself should have a shelf-life of two to three years. By the very nature, implementation plans will become obsolete and new priorities will emerge. Think of it in terms of relative permanence. The position statements are considered to be etched in stone; the strategic priorities are written in ink; and the implementation plans are written in pencil. Too often, completed implementation plans are the impetus for a new strategic plan. It is for this reason that I separate the strategic framework from the implementation plans.

Priorities Within the Priorities

One challenge you are likely to face in the execution of a strategy is competing priorities. An example of competing priorities is when a nonprofit receives a large bequest that was not expected. Should the gift be designated by the board as operational endowment? Or, does this present an opportunity to accelerate the growth of the on-site school? And what about the aging HVAC system, which many of your current donors are not excited about supporting?

By definition, if everything is of the highest priority, you really have no priorities at all. To help with this difficult task of setting the "priorities within the priorities", I have developed a template for differentiating among priorities (see Table 7). Let me be clear: there are no full-proof tools that will allow you to follow the dots to the right decision for the best use of resources.

We know that opportunities and challenges are just as likely to emerge without warning as are the ones we anticipate. Being strategic requires that nonprofits approach the unexpected and the expected with consistency and intentionality. The priorities template is intended to provide a starting point for these deliberations.

Table 7: Differentiating Among Priorities

	Strategic Position	**Capacity Building**
Critical	- Advances a strategic priority - Lost opportunity if no action taken	- Immediate threat to organizational stability - High risk if no action taken
Important	- Advances a strategic priority - Opportunity is not time-sensitive	- Necessary to maintain organizational stability - Eventual risk if no action taken
Desirable	- Advances a strategic priority - A "wish list" opportunity	- Opportunity to enhance organizational stability - Low risk if no action taken

Type of Priority

Strategic Position priorities are related to opportunities for strategic positioning and address: a) program enhancement; b) collaborations and partnerships; c) resource development; and/or, d) community relations.

Capacity Position priorities are related to general organizational stability and address such things as operational capacity and efficiency, leadership succession, staff development, and internal systems.

Nature of Risk[35]

Critical tasks are those that have the potential for immediate and significant consequences.

Important tasks have potential as either a threat or an opportunity but do not require immediate action.

Desirable tasks neither pose an immediate threat to organizational stability nor hamper strategic positioning.

---

[35] Adapted from the work of Derek Lidow.

CONCLUSION

I would like to close by reinforcing a few of the key principles of effective strategy development for nonprofits. First, strategy across the Lifecycle Stages framework—like any advanced conceptual organizer—is intended as a heuristic device rather than a blueprint for action. That is, the lifecycles framework provides a starting point for strategy by identifying the questions that are most relevant to your nonprofit in its current stage of development. Where the answers to those questions take you will depend on a number of factors, both within and outside of your control.

Second, whether viewed as lifecycle stages or strategic phases, the process of organizational development is neither linear nor predictable. My approach to organizational planning is based on my recognition that life can get messy in unpredictable ways. If we begin with conceptual clarity about where we are and where we need to go, we are in a much better position to respond intentionally and thoughtfully to the ambiguity and uncertainty that is inevitable. However, ambiguity on the front end can result in chaos and frustration as your nonprofit is faced with challenges and opportunities, both expected and unexpected.

Because stage or phase-based strategy is not linear, there is no guarantee that any particular nonprofit will successfully move from Startup to Maturity. Aspiration is not destiny. The reality is that a nonprofit can move toward decline at any point along its organizational history. This is because each strategic phase brings its own set of specific challenges to be overcome and developmental tasks to be achieved. Said another way, different types of programs have different comparative advantages at each stage of its lifecycle. For example, the competencies required for a successful program launch will not ensure successful growth, which will depend on the ability to achieve a cost or quality advantage.[36] This fact alone is sufficient cause to compel nonprofits to align their organizational capacity with their strategic aspirations.

Third, it is imperative to sound strategy that the right questions be asked at the right time. A Startup nonprofit, for example, should strive for clarity in its intentions and aspirations as conveyed through its theory of change. At this stage, it is unreasonable to expect the nonprofit to give a meaningful description of its organizational core. By the same token, a Mature organization should be able to reflect on its past and draw lessons to guide it forward. Even though the destination is the same for both the Startup and Mature nonprofit, the starting point for each—that is, the strategic phase within which the organization operates currently—will shape questions that will guide the strategic journey.

The fourth point is related to the strategic plan document. Despite my best attempts, there is no universal

---

[36] Kevin Kearns, *Wise Decision-Making in Uncertain Times*. (Foundation Center, 2006).

template for a strategic framework and implementation plans. And that is okay. The form and presentation of the strategic material should flow from the management style of the CEO and the governance disposition of the board of directors. But please know this: regardless of the format you choose, the effectiveness of the document will hinge on the ability of the strategic priorities that form a bridge between the vision and action. You will have achieved this when everyone associated with the organization will be able to say, after reading the document, "I know what this means for me in my role."

Lastly, strategic thinking trumps strategic planning every time. The strategic framework, used correctly, is a tool that fosters ongoing strategic thinking. The truth is a nonprofit should never have to start from scratch in developing a strategic plan. Just as there is no finish line when it comes to strategic positioning, a strategic framework should never expire. The key is knowing the right questions and when to ask them. I recommend that nonprofits conduct annual reviews of their strategic framework, guided by three basic questions: 1) what were we thinking then? 2) what has happened since? 3) what do we do next?

Done consistently and with focused attention, the strategic thinking of your nonprofit will gain momentum from the continuous cycle of looking backward, looking inward, then looking forward.

AFTERWORD

This book was written in the midst of the COVID-19 pandemic, which has brought with it a way of living and working that is unprecedented for most of us. The disruption caused by this chain of events has proved to be a stress test for businesses, nonprofits included.

One thing that has become clear is the difficulty of trying to think long-term in the midst of an immediate crisis. The time for the ship captain to reconsider the chosen route is not while the ship is taking on water. Eventually, all aspects of the journey need to be scrutinized, including the route, the sturdiness of the ship, and the capabilities of the crew. But these deliberations occur when (and if) the ship is able to return to port safely. In the meantime, the focus is survival.

The pandemic has shown the importance of maintaining the fundamentals of organizational strength. While we are in extreme circumstances at the present, every nonprofit executive and board of directors should be planning for the inevitable disruptions that are likely to occur, regardless of the cause. Like the captain of the sinking ship regretting the chosen route, the proper response to a severe financial crisis is not to wish your nonprofit had built up a larger operating reserve.

BIBLIOGRAPHY

Kearns, Kevin P. "Market Engagement and Competition: Opportunities, Challenges, and the Quest for Comparative Advantage." Wise Decision-Making in Uncertain Times, Dennis Young, editor. Foundation Center (2006).

Lidow, Derek. "A Better Way to Set Strategic Priorities." HBR Guide to Thinking Strategically. Harvard Business Review Press (2019).

McLaughlin, T. Nonprofit Strategic Planning: Decide Where to Be, Plan What to Do. Wiley (2006).

Mintzberg, H. Rise and Fall of Strategic Planning. The Free Press (1994).

Mintzberg, H. Tracking Strategies: Toward a General Theory. Oxford University Press. (2007).

Mintzberg, H. and Waters, J. "Of Strategies, Deliberate and Emergent." Strategic Management Journal, v. 6, pp 257-72 (1985).

Porter, M. "What is Strategy?" Harvard Business Review, November-December (1996).

Schon, D. The Reflective Practitioner: How Professional Think in Action, Ashgate Publishing (1983).

Stevens, Susan K. Nonprofit Lifecycles: Stage-Based Wisdom for Nonprofit Capacity, Stagewise Enterprise, Inc. (2001:2008).

Westley, F., Zimmerman, B., and Patton, M.Q. Getting to Maybe: How the World is Changed. Vintage Canada (2007).

Young, Dennis. Financing Nonprofits: Putting Theory into Practice, Dennis Young, editor, AltaMira Press (2007).

Made in the USA
Monee, IL
19 August 2020